Exercises
to accompany

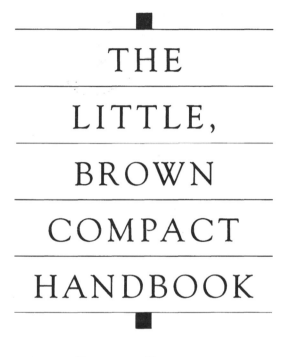

THE

LITTLE,

BROWN

COMPACT

HANDBOOK

FOURTH EDITION

Jane E. Aaron

Longman

New York   San Francisco   Boston
London   Toronto   Sydney   Singapore   Madrid
Mexico City   Munich   Paris   Cape Town   Hong Kong   Montreal

Exercises to accompany
The Little, Brown Compact Handbook, Fourth Edition

Copyright © 2001 by Addison-Wesley Educational Publishers Inc.

ISBN: 0-321-07771-7

2 3 4 5 6 7 8 9 10 — CRW — 03 02 01

PREFACE

The 105 exercises in this book give students a chance to try out what they have learned from *The Little, Brown Compact Handbook*, Fourth edition. The exercises range from revising paragraphs through correcting grammar and punctuation to paraphrasing sources and writing works-cited entries. This edition has an increased number of sentence-combining exercises to provide direct experience working within sentences. With a few exceptions, the work can be completed on the pages of this book. Like actual writing, the exercises are in connected discourse, with sentences building passages on cross-disciplinary topics, such as literature, business practice, and animal behavior.

Each exercise is keyed to the relevant section(s) and page number(s) in *The Little, Brown Compact Handbook*, or LBCH for short, as in this sample exercise heading:

Exercise 1   *LBCH 6a*
Revising a paragraph for unity   *p. 42*

Students who have difficulty with any exercise should read the appropriate text explanation and then try again.

Nearly every exercise includes an example illustrating what's required to complete the exercise and one or more sample answers in the back of the book. These features assist instructors in discussing exercises with students and help those students working independently. These samples and the remaining answers for each exercise appear in a separate answer key, which instructors may reproduce for distribution to students.

Answers are labeled "possible" when the corresponding exercises encourage choice in responding and the given answers are but suggestions. Even for the objective exercises, which more often lend themselves to one response, some users may disagree with some answers. Usage is often flexible, and many rules allow interpretation. The answers here conform to the usage recommended in *The Little, Brown Compact Handbook*.

Contents

PARAGRAPHS

CLARITY AND STYLE

SENTENCE PARTS AND PATTERNS

BASIC GRAMMAR

VERBS

PRONOUNS

SPELLING AND MECHANICS

RESEARCH AND DOCUMENTATION

PARAGRAPHS

Exercise 1   LBCII 6a
Revising a paragraph for unity   p. 42

The following paragraph contains ideas or details that do not support its central idea. Underline the topic sentence in the paragraph and delete the unrelated material.

¹In the southern part of the state, some people still live much as they did a century ago. ²They use coal- or wood-burning stoves for heating and cooking. ³Their homes do not have electricity or indoor bathrooms or running water. ⁴The towns they live in don't receive adequate funding from the state and federal governments, so the schools are poor and in bad shape. ⁵Beside most homes there is a garden where fresh vegetables are gathered for canning. ⁶Small pastures nearby support livestock, including cattle, pigs, horses, and chickens. ⁷Most of the people have cars or trucks, but the vehicles are old and beat-up from traveling on unpaved roads.

Exercise 2   LBCH 6a
Writing a unified paragraph   p. 42

On separate paper or on a computer, develop the following topic sentence into a unified paragraph by using the relevant information in the statements below it. Delete each statement that does not relate directly to the topic, and then rewrite and combine sentences as appropriate. Place the topic sentence in the position that seems most effective to you.

Topic sentence
Mozart's accomplishments in music seem remarkable even today.

Supporting information

Wolfgang Amadeus Mozart was born in 1756 in Salzburg, Austria.
He began composing music at the age of five.
He lived most of his life in Salzburg and Vienna.
His first concert tour of Europe was at the age of six.
On his first tour he played harpsichord, organ, and violin.
He published numerous compositions before reaching adolescence.
He married in 1782.
Mozart and his wife were both poor managers of money.
They were plagued by debts.
Mozart composed over six hundred musical compositions.
His most notable works are his operas, symphonies, quartets, and piano concertos.
He died at the age of thirty-five.

Exercise 3   LBCH 6b
Arranging sentences coherently   p. 32

After the topic sentence (sentence 1), the sentences in the student paragraph below have been deliberately scrambled to make the paragraph inco-
herent. Using the topic sentence and other clues as guides, rearrange the
sentences in the paragraph to form a well-organized coherent unit. Using
the seven sentence numbers, write the correct order on the blank line following the paragraph.

> [1]We hear complaints about the Postal Service all the
> time, but we should not forget what it does *right*. [2]The total
> volume of mail delivered by the Postal Service each year
> makes up almost half the total delivered in all the world. [3]Its
> 70,000 employees handle 140,000,000,000 pieces of mail each
> year. [4]And when was the last time they failed to deliver
> yours? [5]In fact, on any given day the Postal Service delivers
> almost as much mail as the rest of the world combined. [6]That
> huge number means over 2,000,000 pieces per employee and
> over 560 pieces per man, woman, and child in the country.

Exercise 4   LBCH 6b
Using transitional expressions   p. 47

Transitional expressions have been removed from the following paragraph
at the numbered blanks. Fill in each blank with an appropriate transitional

expression (1) to contrast, (2) to intensify, and (3) to show effect. If necessary, consult the list on p. 47 of the text.

All over the country, people are swimming, jogging, weightlifting, dancing, walking, playing tennis—doing anything to keep fit. (1)_____ this school has consistently refused to construct and equip a fitness center. The school has (2)_____ refused to open existing athletic facilities to all students, not just those playing organized sports. (3)_____ students have no place to exercise except in their rooms and on dangerous public roads.

Exercise 5   LBCH 6b
Writing a coherent paragraph   p. 44

On separate paper or on a computer, write a coherent paragraph from the following information, combining and rewriting sentences as necessary. First, begin the paragraph with the topic sentence given and arrange the supporting sentences in a climactic order. Then combine and rewrite the supporting sentences, helping the reader see connections by introducing parallelism, repetition and restatement, pronouns, consistency, and transitional expressions.

Topic sentence
Hypnosis is far superior to drugs for relieving tension.

Supporting information
Hypnosis has none of the dangerous side effects of the drugs that relieve tension.
Tension-relieving drugs can cause weight loss or gain, illness, or even death.
Hypnosis is nonaddicting.
Most of the drugs that relieve tension do foster addiction.
Tension-relieving drugs are expensive.
Hypnosis is inexpensive even for people who have not mastered self-hypnosis.

Exercise 6
Analyzing and revising skimpy paragraphs

LBCH 6c
p. 48

The following paragraphs are not well developed. Analyze them, looking especially for general statements that lack support or leave questions in your mind. Then, on separate paper or on a computer, rewrite one into a well-developed paragraph, supplying your own concrete details or examples.

1. One big difference between successful and unsuccessful teachers is the quality of communication. A successful teacher is sensitive to students' needs and excited by the course subject. In contrast, an unsuccessful teacher seems uninterested in students and bored by the subject.

2. Gestures are one of our most important means of communication. We use them instead of speech. We use them to supplement the words we speak. And we use them to communicate some feelings or meanings that words cannot adequately express.

3. I've discovered that a word processor can do much – but not everything – to help me improve my writing. I can easily make changes and try out different versions of a paper. But I still must do the hard work of revising.

CLARITY AND STYLE

Rewrite the following sentences so that their subjects and verbs identify their key actors and actions. (Answers to the first two items appear at the back of the book.)

> EXAMPLE:
> The issue of students making a competition over grades is a reason why their focus on learning may be lost.
>
> <u>Students</u> who compete over grades <u>may lose</u> their focus on learning.

1. The work of many heroes was crucial in helping to emancipate the slaves.

2. The contribution of Harriet Tubman, an escaped slave herself, included the guidance of hundreds of other slaves to freedom on the Underground Railroad.

3. A return to slavery was risked by Tubman or possibly death.

4. During the Civil War she was also a carrier of information from the South to the North.

5. After the war needy former slaves were helped by Tubman's raising of money for refugees.

Exercise 8   **LBCH 11b**
Sentence combining: Beginnings and endings   *p. 119*

Locate the main idea in each group of sentences below. Then combine each group into a single sentence that emphasizes that idea by placing it at the beginning or the end. For sentences 2-5, determine the position of the main idea by considering its relation to the previous sentences: if the main idea picks up a topic that's already been introduced, place it at the beginning; if it adds new information, place it at the end. (Answers to the first two items appear at the back of this book).

EXAMPLE:

The storm blew roofs off buildings. It caused extensive damage. It knocked down many trees. It severed power lines.

Main idea at beginning: The storm caused extensive damage, blowing roofs off buildings, knocking down many trees, and severing power lines.

Main idea at end: Blowing roofs off buildings, knocking down many trees, and severing power lines, the storm caused extensive damage.

1. Pat Taylor strode into the room. The room was packed. He greeted students called "Taylor's Kids." He nodded to their parents and teachers.

2. This was a wealthy Louisiana oilman. He had promised his "Kids" free college educations. He was determined to make higher education available to all qualified but disadvantaged students.

3. The students welcomed Taylor. Their voices joined in singing. They sang "You Are the Wind Beneath My Wings." Their faces beamed with hope. Their eyes flashed with self-confidence.

4. The students had thought college education was beyond their dreams. It seemed too costly. It seemed too demanding.

Exercise 9   LBCH 11c
Sentence combining: Coordination   p. 115

Combine sentences in the following passages to coordinate related ideas in the way that seems most effective to you. You will have to supply coordinating conjunctions or conjunctive adverbs and the appropriate punctuation. (A revision of the first passage appears in the back of this book.)

1. Many chronic misspellers do not have the time to master spelling rules. They may not have the motivation. They may rely on dictionaries to catch misspellings. Most dictionaries list words under their correct spellings. One kind of dictionary is designed for chronic misspellers. It lists each word under its common misspellings. It then provides the correct spelling. It also provides the definition.

2. Henry Hudson was an English explorer. He captained ships for the Dutch East India Company. On a voyage in 1610 he passed by Greenland. He sailed into a great bay in today's northern Canada. He thought he and his sailors could winter there. The cold was terrible. Food ran out. The sailors mutinied. The sailors cast Hudson adrift in a small boat. Eight others were also in the boat. Hudson and his companions perished.

Exercise 10   LBCH 11d
Sentence combining: Subordination   p. 121

Combine each of the following pairs of sentences twice, each time using one of the subordinate structures in brackets to make a single sentence. You will have to add, delete, change, and rearrange words. (The first two items are answered in the back of this book.)

Example:

During the late eighteenth century, workers carried beverages in brightly colored bottles. The bottles had cork stoppers. (*Clause beginning that. Phrase beginning with.*)

During the late eighteenth century, workers carried beverages in brightly colored bottles <u>that had cork stoppers</u>.

During the late eighteenth century, workers carried beverages in brightly colored bottles <u>with cork stoppers</u>.

1. The bombardier beetle sees an enemy. It shoots out a jet of chemicals to protect itself. (*Clause beginning when. Phrase beginning seeing.*)

2. The beetle's spray is very potent. It consists of hot and irritating chemicals. (*Phrase beginning consisting. Phrase beginning of.*)

3. The spray's two chemicals are stored separately in the beetle's body and mixed in the spraying gland. The chemicals resemble a nerve-gas weapon. (*Phrase beginning stored. Clause beginning which.*)

4. The tip of the beetle's abdomen sprays the chemicals. The tip revolves like a turret on a World War II bomber. (*Phrase beginning revolving. Phrase beginning spraying.*)

5. The beetle defeats most of its enemies. It is still eaten by spiders and birds. (*Clause beginning although. Phrase beginning except.*)

Exercise 11   **LBCH 11c, 11d**
Revising: Coordination and subordination   *pp. 119-123*

The following paragraph consists entirely of simple sentences. Use coordination and subordination to combine sentences in the way you think is most effective to emphasize main ideas. (A revision of the first three sentences appears at the back of this book.)

Sir Walter Raleigh personified the Elizabethan Age. That was the period of Elizabeth I's rule of England. The period occurred in the last half of the sixteenth century. Raleigh was a courtier and poet. He was also an explorer and entrepreneur. Supposedly, he gained Queen Elizabeth's favor. He did this by throwing his cloak beneath her feet at the right moment. She was just about to step over a puddle. There is no evidence for this story. It does illustrate Raleigh's dramatic and dynamic personality. His energy drew others to him. He was one of Elizabeth's favorites. She supported him. She also dispensed favors to him. However, he lost his queen's good will. Without her permission he seduced one of her maids of honor. He eventually married the maid of honor. Elizabeth died. Then her successor imprisoned Raleigh in the Tower of London. Her successor was James I. Raleigh was charged falsely with treason. He was released after thirteen years. He was arrested again two years later on the old treason charges. At the age of sixty-six he was beheaded.

Exercise 12   **LBCH 12**
Sentence combining: Parallelism   *p. 123*

Combine each group of sentences below into one concise sentence in which parallel elements appear in parallel structures. You will have to add, delete, change, and rearrange words. Each item has more than one possible answer. (A revision of the first item appears at the back of this book.)

Example:

The new process works smoothly. It is efficient too.

The new process works smoothly <u>and efficiently</u>.

1. People can develop post-traumatic stress disorder (PTSD). They develop it after experiencing a dangerous situation. They will also have felt fear for their survival.

   People can develop post-traumatic disorder after experiencing a dangerous situation and fearing for their survival.

2. The disorder can be triggered by a wide variety of events. Combat is a typical cause. Similarly, natural disasters can result in PTSD. Some people experience PTSD after a hostage situation.

   The disorder can be triggered by a wide variety of events

3. PTSD can occur immediately after the stressful incident. Or it may not appear until many years later.

4. Sometimes people with PTSD will act irrationally. Moreover, they often become angry.

5. Other symptoms include dreaming that one is reliving the experience. They include hallucinating that one is back in the terrifying place. In another symptom one imagines that strangers are actually one's former torturers.

Exercise 13   LBCH 12
Revising: Parallelism   *p. 124*

Revise the following paragraph to create parallelism wherever it is required
for grammar or for coherence. (A revision of the first two sentences
appears at the back of this book.)

The great white shark has an undeserved bad reputation.
Many people consider the great white not only swift and powerful but also to be a cunning and cruel predator on humans.
However, scientists claim that the great white attacks humans
not by choice but as a result of chance. To a shark, our behavior in the water is similar to that of porpoises, seals, and sea
lions—the shark's favorite foods. These sea mammals are both
agile enough and can move fast enough to evade the shark.
Thus the shark must attack with swiftness and noiselessly to
surprise the prey and giving it little chance to escape.
Humans become the shark's victims not because the shark has
any preference or hatred of humans but because humans can
neither outswim nor can they outmaneuver the shark. If the
fish were truly a cruel human-eater, it would prolong the terror
of its attacks, perhaps by circling or bumping into its intended
victims before they were attacked.

Exercise 14   LBCH 13
Revising: Variety   *p. 126*

The following paragraph consists entirely of simple sentences that begin
with their subjects. As appropriate, vary sentences so that the paragraph is
more readable and its important ideas stand out clearly. You will have to
delete, add, change, and rearrange words. (A revision of the first two sentences appears at the back of this book.)

The Italian volcano Vesuvius had been dormant for many

years. It then exploded on August 24 in the year AD 79. The

ash, pumice, and mud from the volcano buried two busy
~~Two busy town, The most famous Pompeii and Hercula~~
towns. Herculaneum is one. The more famous is Pompeii.
~~were buried by the ash, pumice and mud from the~~
The ruins of both towns, lay undiscovered for many centuries. ~~vulca~~
~~till~~
Herculaneum and Pompeii were discovered in 1709 and 1748,

respectively. The excavation of Pompeii was the more system-

atic. It was the occasion for initiating modern methods of

conservation and restoration. Herculaneum was simply looted

of its most valuable finds. It was then left to disintegrate.

Pompeii appears much as it did before the eruption. A luxuri-

ous house opens onto a lush central garden. An election

poster decorates a wall. A dining table is set for breakfast.

Exercise 15   LBCH 14a
Revising: Appropriate words   *p. 131*

Rewrite the following sentences as needed for standard written English.
Consult a dictionary to determine whether particular words are appropriate
and to find suitable substitutes. (The first three items are answered in the
back of this book.)

Example:

If negotiators get hyper during contract discussions, they may mess up
chances for a settlement.

If negotiators <u>become excited or upset</u> during contract discussions, they
may <u>harm</u> chances for a settlement.

1. Acquired immune deficiency syndrome (AIDS) is a major deal all over
   the world.

2. The disease gets around primarily by sexual intercourse, exchange of bodily fluids, shared needles, and blood transfusions.

3. Those who think the disease is limited to homos and druggies are quite mistaken.

4. Stats suggest that one in every five hundred college kids carries the virus.

5. A person with AIDS does not deserve to be subjected to exclusionary behavior or callousness on the part of his fellow citizens. Instead, he has the necessity for all the compassion, medical care, and financial assistance due those who are in the extremity of illness.

6. An AIDS victim often sees a team of doctors or a single doctor with a specialized practice.

7. The doctor may help his patients by obtaining social services for them as well as by providing medical care.

8. The AIDS sufferer who loses his job may need public assistance.

9. For someone who is very ill, a full-time nurse may be necessary. She can administer medications and make the sick person as comfortable as possible.

10. Some people with AIDS have insurance, but others lack the bread for premiums.

Exercise 16   LBCH 14b
Revising: Denotation   p. 136

Revise any underlined word below that is not used according to its established denotation. Circle any underlined word that is used correctly. Consult a dictionary if you are uncertain of a word's precise meaning. (The first item is answered in the back of this book.)

Example:

Sam and Dave are going to Bermuda and Hauppauge, <u>respectfully</u>, for spring vacation.

Sam and Dave are going to Bermuda and Hauppauge, <u>respectively</u>, for spring vacation.

1. Maxine Hong Kingston was <u>rewarded</u> many prizes for her first two books, *The Woman Warrior* and *China Men*.

2. Kingston <u>sites</u> her mother's tales about ancestors and ancient Chinese customs as the sources of these memoirs.

3. In her childhood Kingston was greatly <u>effected</u> by her mother's tale about a pregnant aunt who was <u>ostracized</u> by villagers.

4. The aunt gained <u>avengeance</u> by drowning herself in the village's water supply.

5. Kingston decided to make her nameless relative <u>infamous</u> by giving her <u>immortality</u> in *The Woman Warrior*.

Exercise 17   *LBCH 14b*
Considering the connotations of words   *p. 138*

Fill the blank in each sentence below with the most appropriate word from the list in brackets. Consult a dictionary to be sure of your choice. (The first item is answered in the back of this book.)

Example:

Channel 5 _____ Oshu the winner before the polls closed. (*advertised, declared, broadcast, promulgated*)

Channel 5 <u>declared</u> Oshu the winner before the polls closed.

1. AIDS is a serious health _____. (*problem, worry, difficulty, plight*)

2. Once the virus has entered the blood system, it _____ T-cells. (*murders, destroys, slaughters, executes*)

3. The _____ of T-cells is to combat infections. (*ambition, function, aim, goal*)

4. Without enough T-cells, the body is nearly _____ against infections. (*defenseless, hopeless, desperate*)

5. To prevent exposure to the disease, one should be especially _____ in sexual relationships. (*chary, circumspect, cautious, calculating*)

Exercise 18   **LBCH 14b**
Revising: Concrete and specific words   *p. 139*

Make the following paragraph vivid by expanding the sentences with
appropriate details of your own choosing. Substitute concrete and specific
words for the underlined abstract and general ones. (A revision of the first
sentence appears in the back of this book.)

I remember <u>clearly</u> how <u>awful</u> I felt the first time I <u>attend-
ed</u> Mrs. Murphy's second-grade class. I had <u>recently</u> moved
from a <u>small</u> town in Missouri to a <u>crowded</u> suburb of Chicago.
My new school looked <u>big</u> from the outside and seemed <u>dark</u>
inside as I <u>walked</u> down the <u>long</u> corridor toward the class-
room. The class was <u>noisy</u> as I neared the door; but when I
<u>entered</u>, <u>everyone</u> became <u>quiet</u> and <u>looked</u> at me. I felt
<u>uncomfortable</u> and <u>wanted</u> a place to hide. However, in a
<u>loud</u> voice Mrs. Murphy <u>directed</u> me to the front of the room
to introduce myself.

Exercise 19   **LBCH 14b**
Using prepositions in idioms   *p. 140*

Insert the preposition that correctly completes each idiom in the following
sentences. Consult a dictionary or the list on page 141 of the text as needed. (A revision of the first item appears in the back of this book.)

Example:

I disagree _____ many feminists who say women should not be
homemakers.

I disagree <u>with</u> many feminists who say women should not be homemakers.

1. As Mark and Lana waited _____ the justice of the peace, they
    seemed oblivious_____ the other people in the lobby.

2. But Mark inferred _____ Lana's glance at a handsome man that she was no longer occupied _____ him alone.

3. Angry _____ Lana, Mark charged her _____ not loving him enough to get married.

4. Impatient _____ Mark's childish behavior, Lana disagreed _____ his interpretation of her glance.

5. They decided that if they could differ so violently _____ a minor incident, they should part _____ each other.

Exercise 20   LBCH 14b
Revising: Trite expressions   p. 143

Revise the following sentences to eliminate trite expressions. (A revision of the first sentence appears in the back of this book.)

Example:

The basketball team had almost seized victory, but it faced the test of truth in the last quarter of the game.

The basketball team <u>seemed about to win</u>, but the <u>real test</u> came in the last quarter of the game.

1. The disastrous consequences of the war have shaken the small nation to its roots.

2. Prices for food have shot sky high, and citizens have sneaking suspicions that others are making a killing on the black market.

3. Medical supplies are so few and far between that even civilians who are as sick as dogs cannot get treatment.

4. With most men fighting or injured or killed, women have had to bite the bullet and bear the men's burden in farming and manufacturing.

4. Last but not least, the war's heavy drain on the nation's pocketbook has left the economy in a shambles.

Exercise 21   **LBCH 16a, 16b**
Revising: Subjects and verbs;
empty words and phrases   **p. 145, 147**

Revise the following sentences to achieve conciseness focusing on subjects and verbs and by by cutting or reducing empty words and phrases. (A revision of the first sentence appears in the back of this book.)

Example:

I made college my destination because of many factors, but most of all because of the fact that I want a career in medicine.

I came to college mainly because I want a career in medicine.

1. Gerrymandering refers to a situation in which the lines of a voting district are redrawn so that a particular party or ethnic group has benefits.

2. The name is a reference to the fact that Elbridge Gerry, the governor of Massachusetts in 1812, redrew voting districts in Essex County.

3. On the map one new district was seen to resemble something in the nature of a salamander.

4. Upon seeing the map, a man who was for all intents and purposes a critic of Governor Gerry's administration cried out, "Gerrymander!"

5. At the present time, changes may be made in the character of a district's voting pattern by a political group by gerrymandering to achieve the exclusion of the rival groups' supporters.

Exercise 22   **LBCH 16c**
Revising: Unnecessary repetition   *p. 148*

Revise the following sentences to achieve conciseness. Concentrate on eliminating repetition and redundancy. (A revision of the first sentence appears in the back of this book.)

Example:

Because the circumstances surrounding the cancellation of classes were murky and unclear, the editor of the student newspaper assigned a staff reporter to investigate and file a report on the circumstances.

Because the circumstances leading to the cancellation of classes were <u>unclear</u>, the editor of the student newspaper assigned a <u>staffer</u> to investigate and <u>report the story</u>.

1. Some Vietnam veterans coming back to the United States after their tours of duty in Vietnam had problems readjusting again to life in America.

2. Afflicted with post-traumatic stress disorder, a psychological disorder that sometimes arises after a trauma, some veterans had psychological problems that caused them to have trouble holding jobs and maintaining relationships.

3. Some who used to use drugs in Vietnam could not break their drug habits after they returned back to the United States.

4. The few Veterans who committed crimes and violent acts gained so much notoriety and fame that many Americans thought all veterans were crazy, insane maniacs.

5. As a result of such stereotyping of Vietnam-era veterans, veterans are included into the same antidiscrimination laws that protect other victims of discrimination.

Exercise 23   **LBCH 16**
Revising: Conciseness   **p. 145**

Rewrite each passage below into a single concise sentence, using the techniques described in pp. 145 - 150 of the text. (A revision of the first sentence appears in the back of this book.)

Example:

He was taking some exercise in the park. Then several thugs were suddenly ahead in his path.

He was <u>exercising</u> [or <u>jogging</u> or <u>strolling</u>] in the park <u>when</u> several thugs suddenly <u>loomed</u> in his path.

1. Chewing gum was originally introduced to the United States by Antonio Lopez de Santa Anna. He was the Mexican general.

2. After he had been defeated by the Texans in 1845, the general, who was exiled, made the choice to settle in New York.

3. A piece of chicle had been stashed by the general in his baggage. Chicle is the dried milky sap of the Mexican sapodilla tree.

4. There was more of this resin brought into the country by Santa Anna's friend Thomas Adams. Adams had a plan to make rubber.

5. The plan failed. Then the occasion arose for Adams to get a much more successful idea on the basis of the use to which the resin was put by General Santa Anna. That is, Adams decided to make a gum that could be chewed.

Exercise 24   **LBCH 16**
Revising: Conciseness   *p. 145*

Make the following passage as concise as possible. Be merciless. (A revision of the first sentence appears in the back of this book.)

At the end of a lengthy line of reasoning, he came to the

conclusion that the situation with carcinogens [cancer-causing

substances] should be regarded as similar to the situation with the automobile. Rather than giving in to an irrational fear of cancer, we should consider all aspects of the problem in a balanced and dispassionate frame of mind, making a total of the benefits received from potential carcinogens (plastics, pesticides, and other similar products) and measuring said total against the damage done by such products. This is the nature of most discussions about the automobile. Rather than responding irrationally to the visual, aural, and air pollution caused by automobiles, we have decided to live with them (while simultaneously working to improve on them) for the benefits brought to society as a whole.

SENTENCE PARTS
AND PATTERNS

BASIC GRAMMAR

Exercise 25   **LBCH 17**
Identifying nouns, verbs, and pronouns   **p. 154**

In the following sentences identify all words functioning as nouns with N, all words functioning as verbs with V, and all pronouns with P. (The first item is answered in the back of this book.)

> *Example:*
>
> We took the tour through the museum.
> P   V   N   N
> <u>We</u> <u>took</u> the <u>tour</u> through the <u>museum.</u>

The trees died.

They caught a disease.

The disease was a fungus.

It ruined a grove that was treasured.

Our great-grandfather planted the grove in the last century.

Exercise 26   **LBCH 17**
Using nouns and verbs   **p. 154**

The following words can be used as both nouns and verbs. Write sentences that use them both ways. (The first sentence is answered in the back of this book.)

> *Example:*
>
> fly
>
> The <u>fly</u> sat on the meat loaf. [Noun] The planes <u>fly</u> low. [Verb]

wish_____

_____

_____

tie_____

_____

_____

swing_____

_____

_____

mail_____

_____

_____

label_____

_____

_____

whistle_____

_____

_____

glue_____

_____

_____

Exercise 27   **LBCH 17d**
Identifying adjectives and adverbs   *p. 158*

Identify the adjectives and adverbs in the following sentences. (The first item is answered in the back of this book.)

Example:

The red barn sat uncomfortably among modern buildings.

    adjective   adverb   adjective
The <u>red</u> barn sat <u>uncomfortably</u> among <u>modern</u> buildings.

1. The icy rain created glassy patches on the roads.

2. Happily, children played in the slippery streets.

3. Fortunately, no cars ventured out.

4. Wise parents stayed indoors, where they could be warm and dry.

5. The dogs slept soundly near the warm radiators.

Exercise 28   **LBCH 17e, 19a**
Sentence combining: Prepositional phrases   *pp. 158, 164*

Combine each group of sentences below into one sentence that includes one or two prepositional phrases. You will have to add, delete, and rearrange words. Some items have more than one possible answer. (A revision of the first item appears in the back of this book.)

Example:

I will start working. The new job will pay the minimum wage.

I will start working at a new job for the minimum wage.

1. The slow loris protects itself well. Its habitat is Southeast Asia. It possesses a poisonous chemical.

2. To frighten predators, the loris exudes the chemical. The chemical comes from a gland. The gland is on the loris's upper arm.

3. The loris's chemical is highly toxic. The chemical is not like a skunk's spray. Even small quantities of the chemical are toxic.

4. A tiny dose can affect a human. The dose would get in the mouth. The human would be sent into shock.

5. Predators probably can sense the toxin. They detect it at a distance. They use their nasal organs.

Exercise 29   LBCH 18
Identifying subjects and predicates   *p. 161*

Identify the subject and the predicate of each sentence below. (The first item is answered in the back of this book.)

Example:

An important scientist spoke at commencement.

            subject   predicate
An important scientist | spoke at commencement.

1. The leaves fell.

2. October ends soon.

3. The orchard owners made apple cider.

4. They examined each apple carefully before using it.

5. Over a hundred people will buy cider at the roadside stand.

Exercise 30   **LBCH 18b**
Identifying sentence patterns   *p. 162*

In the following sentences, identify each verb as intransitive, transitive, or linking. Then identify each direct object (DO), indirect object (IO), subject complement (SC), and object complement (OC). (The first item is answered in the back of this book.)

Example:

Children give their parents both headaches and pleasures.

Verb: *Give* is transitive.

          IO   DO   DO
Children give their <u>parents</u> both <u>headaches</u> and <u>pleasures</u>.

1. Many people find New Orleans exciting.
   Verb:

2. Tourists flock there each year.
   Verb:

3. Usually they visit the French Quarter first.
   Verb:

4. The Quarter's old buildings are magnificent.
   Verb:

5. In the Quarter, artists sell tourists their paintings.
   Verb:

Exercise 31   **LBCH 19a**
Identifying verbals and verbal phrases   *p. 164*

The following sentences contain participles, gerunds, and infinitives, as well as participial, gerund, and infinitive phrases. First underline each verbal or verbal phrase. Then indicate whether it is used as an adjective, an adverb, or a noun. (A revision of the first item is found in the back of this book.)

Example:

Laughing, the talk-show host prodded her guest to talk.

Adjective   Adverb
<u>Laughing</u>, the talk-show host prodded her guest <u>to talk</u>.

1. Written in 1850 by Nathaniel Hawthorne, *The Scarlet Letter* tells the story of Hester Prynne.

2. Shunned by the community, Hester endures her loneliness.

3. Hester is humble enough to withstand her Puritan neighbors' cutting remarks.

4. Despite the cruel treatment, the determined young woman refuses to leave her home.

5. By living a life of patience and unselfishness, Hester eventually becomes the community's angel.

Exercise 32   LBCH 19a
Sentence combining: Verbals and verbal phrases   p. 165

Combine each pair of sentences below into one sentence. You will have to add, delete, change, and rearrange words. Each item has more than one possible answer. (A revision of the first item appears in the back of this book.)

Example:

My father took pleasure in mean pranks. For instance, he hid the neighbor's cat.

My father took pleasure in mean pranks such as <u>hiding the neighbor's cat</u>.

1. Air pollution is a health problem. It affects millions of Americans.

2. The air has been polluted mainly by industries and automobiles. It contains toxic chemicals.

3. Environmentalists pressure politicians. They think politicians should pass stricter laws.

4. Many politicians waver. They are not necessarily against environmentalism.

5. The problems are too complex. They cannot be solved easily.

Exercise 33   **LBCH 19b**
Identifying subordinate clauses   *p. 166*

Underline the subordinate clauses in the following sentences. Then indicate whether each is used as an adjective, an adverb, or a noun. If the clause is a noun, indicate what function it performs in the sentence. (The first item is answered in the back of this book.)

Example:

The article explained how one could build an underground house.

Noun (direct object of <u>explained</u>)
The article explained <u>how one could build an underground house</u>.

1. Scientists who want to catch the slightest signals from space use extremely sensitive receivers.

2. Even though they have had to fight for funding, these scientists have persisted in their research.

3. The research is called SETI, which stands for Search for Extraterrestrial Intelligence.

4. The theory is that intelligent beings in space are trying to get in touch with us.

5. The challenge is to guess what frequency these beings would use to send signals.

Exercise 34   LBCH 19b
Sentence combining: Subordinate clauses   p. 166

Combine each pair of main clauses below into one sentence. Use either subordinating conjunctions or relative pronouns as appropriate. You will have to add, delete, and rearrange words. Each item has more than one possible answer. (An answer to the first item appears in the back of this book.)

Example:

She did not have her tire irons with her. She could not change her bicycle tire.

<u>Because</u> she did not have her tire irons with her, she could not change her bicycle tire.

1. Moviegoers expect something. Movie sequels should be as exciting as the original films.

2. A few sequels are good films. Most are poor imitations of the originals.

3. A sequel to a blockbuster film arrives in the theater. Crowds quickly line up to see it.

4. Viewers pay to see the same villains and heroes. They remember these characters fondly.

5. Afterward, viewers often grumble about filmmakers. The filmmakers rehash tired plots and characters.

Exercise 35   LBCH 20
Identifying sentence types   p. 168

In the following sentences, underline each main clause once and draw a double underline under each subordinate clause. Then identify each sentence as simple, compound, complex, or compound-complex. (The first item is answered in the back of this book.)

Example:

The police began patrolling more often when crime in the neighborhood increased.

The police began patrolling more often when crime in the neighborhood increased. [Complex.]

1. Joseph Pulitzer endowed the Pulitzer Prizes.

2. Pulitzer, incidentally, was the publisher of the New York newspaper *The World*.

3. Although the first prizes were for journalism and letters only, Pulitzers are now awarded in music and other areas.

4. For example, Berke Breathed won for his *Bloom County* comic strip, and Roger Reynolds won for his musical composition *Whispers out of Time*.

5. Although only one prize is usually awarded in each category, in 1989 Taylor Branch's *Parting the Waters* won a history prize, and it shared the honor with James M. McPherson's *Battle Cry of Freedom*.

Exercise 36   LBCH 20
Sentence combining: Sentence types   p. 168

Combine each set of simple sentences below to produce the kind of sentence specified in brackets. You will have to add, delete, change, and rearrange words. (A revision of the first item appears in the back of this book.)

Example:

The traffic passed the house. It never stopped. [Complex.]

The traffic that passed the house never stopped.

1. Recycling takes time. It reduces garbage in landfills. [Compound.]

2. People begin to recycle. They generate much less trash. [Complex.]

3. White tissues and paper towels biodegrade more easily than dyed ones. People still buy dyed papers. [Complex.]

4. The cans are aluminum. They bring recyclers good money. [Simple.]

5. Environmentalists have hope. Perhaps more communities will recycle newspaper and glass. Many citizens refuse to participate. [Compound-complex.]

VERBS

Exercise 37   **LBCH 21a**
Using irregular verbs   **p. 170**

For each irregular verb in brackets, give either the past tense or the past participle, as appropriate, and identify the form you use. (The first item is answered in the back of this book.)

Example:

Though we had [*hide*] the cash box, it was [*steal*].

Though we had <u>hidden</u> the cash box, it was <u>stolen</u>. [Two past participles.]

1. The world population has [grow] by two-thirds of a billion people in less than a decade.

2. Recently it [break] the 6 billion mark.

3. Experts have [draw] pictures of a crowded future.

4. They predict that the world population may have [slide] up to as much as 10 billion by the year 2050.

5. Though the food supply [rise] in the last decade, the share to each person [fall].

Exercise 38   LBCH 21b
Distinguishing sit/set, lie/lay, rise/raise   p. 173

Underline the correct verb from the pair given in brackets. (The first item is answered in the back of this book.)

Example:

After I washed all the windows, I [lay, laid] down the squeegee and then I [sat, set] the table.

After I washed all the windows, I <u>laid</u> down the squeegee and then I <u>set</u> the table.

1. Yesterday afternoon the child [lay, laid] down for a nap.

2. The child has been [raised, rose] by her grandparents.

3. Most days her grandfather has [set, sat] with her, reading her stories.

4. She has [risen, raised] at dawn most mornings.

5. Her toys were [laying, lying] out on the floor.

Exercise 39   LBCH 21c
Using -s and -ed verb endings   p. 173

Supply the correct form of each verb in brackets. Be careful to include -s
(and –ed or -d) endings where they are needed for standard English. (A
revision of the first item appears in the back of this book.)

A teacher sometimes [ask] too much of a student. In

high school I was once [punish] for being sick. I had [miss]

some school, and I [realize] that I would fail a test unless I

had a chance to make up the classwork. I [discuss] the

problem with the teacher, but he said I was [suppose] to

make up the work while I was sick. At that, I [walk] out

of the class. I [receive] a failing grade then, but it did not

change my attitude. Today I still balk when a teacher

[make] unreasonable demands or [expect] miracles.

Exercise 40   LBCH 21d
Using helping verbs   p. 174

Add helping verbs in the following sentences where they are needed for
standard English. (The first item is answered in the back of this book.)

1. Each year thousands of new readers been discovering Agatha Christie's
    mysteries.

2. The books written by a prim woman who had worked as a nurse during
    World War I.

3. Christie never expected that her play *The Mousetrap* be performed for
    decades.

4. During her life Christie always complaining about movie versions of
    her stories.

5. Readers of her stories been delighted to be baffled by her.

Exercise 41   LBCH 21d
Revising: Helping verbs plus main verbs (ESL)   p. 174

Revise the following sentences so that helping verbs and main verbs are used correctly. Circle the number of any sentence that is already correct. (The first item is answered in the back of this book.)

Example:

The college testing service has test as many as 500 students at one time.

The college testing service has <u>tested</u> as many as 500 students at one time.

1. A report from the Bureau of the Census has confirm a widening gap between rich and poor.

2. As suspected, the percentage of people below the poverty level did increased over the last decade.

3. More than 17 percent of the population is make 5 percent of all the income.

4. About 1 percent of the population will keeping an average of $500,000 apiece after taxes.

5. The other 99 percent all together may retain about $300,000.

6. More than 80 percent of American families will may make less than $65,000 per family this year.

7. Fewer than 5 percent of families could to make more than $110,000 per family.

8. At the same time that the gap is widen, those in the 80 percent category are work longer hours.

9. Many workers once might have change jobs to increase their pay.

10. Now these workers are remain with the jobs they have.

Exercise 42   LBCH 21e
Revising: Verbs plus gerunds or infinitives (ESL)   *p. 179*

Revise the following sentences so that gerunds or infinitives are used correctly with verbs. Circle the number preceding any sentence that is already correct. (The first item is answered in the back of this book.)

Example:

A politician cannot avoid to alienate some voters.

A politician cannot avoid <u>alienating</u> some voters.

1. A program called HELP Wanted tries to make citizens to take action on behalf of American competitiveness.

2. Officials working on this program hope improving education for work.

3. American businesses find that their workers need learning to read.

4. In the next ten years the United States expects facing a shortage of 350,000 scientists.

5. HELP Wanted suggests creating a media campaign.

Exercise 43   LBCH 21f
Revising: Verbs plus particles (ESL)   p. 181

Identify any two- or three-word verbs in the sentences below, and indicate whether each is separable (S) or inseparable (I). Then fill the blank with the correct option for placing nouns or pronouns with verbs and particles. Consult an (ESL) dictionary if necessary. (The first item is answered in the back of this book.)

Example:

Hollywood producers never seem to come up with entirely new plots, but they also never _____ to present the old ones.

    a. run out of new ways
    b. run new ways out of
    c. Either a or b

Hollywood producers never seem to <u>come up with</u> (I) entirely new plots, but they also never <u>(a) run out of new ways</u> to present the old ones.

American movies treat everything from going out with someone to making up an ethnic identity, but few people _____ .

    a. look into their significance
    b. look their significance into
    c. Either a or b

2. While some viewers stay away from topical films, others _____ simply because a movie has sparked debate.

    a. turn up at the theater
    b. turn at the theater up
    c. Either a or b

3. Some movies aroused such responses that theaters were obliged to
    _____.
    a. throw out rowdy spectators
    b. throw rowdy spectators out
    c. Either a or b

4. Filmmakers have always been eager to _____ to the public.
    a. point out their influence
    b. point their influence out
    c. Either a or b

5. Everyone agrees that filmmakers will _____ , if only because it
    can fill up theaters.
    a. keep on creating controversy
    b. keep creating controversy on
    c. Either a or b

Exercise 44   LBCH 22e
Adjusting tense sequence: Past or past perfect tense   p. 186

The tenses in each sentence below are in correct sequence. Change the
tense of one verb as instructed. Then change the tense of infinitives, participles, and other verbs to restore correct sequence. (The first item is
answered in the back of this book.)

    Example:

    He will call when he reaches his destination. (Change *will call* to
    called.)

    He <u>called</u> when he <u>reached</u> [or <u>had reached</u>] his destination.

1. Diaries that Adolf Hitler is supposed to have written have surfaced in
    Germany. (Change *have surfaced* to *had surfaced.*)

2. Many people believe that the diaries are authentic because a well-known historian has declared them so. (Change *believe* to *believed.*)

3. However, the historian's evaluation has been questioned by other authorities, who call the diaries forgeries. (Change *has been questioned* to *was questioned.*)

4. They claim, among other things, that the paper is not old enough to have been used by Hitler. (Change *claim* to *claimed.*)

5. Eventually, the doubters will win the debate because they have the best evidence. (Change *will win* to *won.*)

Exercise 45   **LBCH 22e**
Revising: Tense sequence with conditional
sentences (ESL)   *p. 187*

Supply the appropriate tense for each verb in brackets below. (The first item is answered in the back of this book.)

Example:

If Babe Ruth or Jim Thorpe [be] athletes today, they [remind] us that even sports heroes must contend with a harsh reality.

If Babe Ruth or Jim Thorpe <u>were</u> athletes today, they <u>might</u> [or <u>could</u> or <u>would</u>] remind us that even sports heroes must contend with a harsh reality.

1. When an athlete [turn] professional, he or she commits to a grueling regimen of mental and physical training.

2. If athletes [be] less committed, they [disappoint] teammates, fans, and themselves.

3. If professional athletes [be] very lucky, they may play until age forty.

4. Unless an athlete achieves celebrity status, he or she [have] few employment choices after retirement.

5. If professional sports [be] less risky, athletes [have] longer careers and more choices after retirement.

Exercise 46   LBCH 22e
Using verb tenses in indirect quotations (ESL)   p. 189

Each passage below comes from the British essayist Charles Lamb (1775-1834). Indirectly quote each passage in a sentence of your own, using the words given in brackets. (The first item is answered in the back of this book.)

Example:

"The greatest pleasure I know is to do a good action by stealth and to have it found out by accident." (*Charles Lamb said that....*)

Charles Lamb said that the greatest pleasure <u>he knew was</u> to do a good action by stealth and to have it found out by accident.

1. "Coleridge holds that a man cannot have a pure mind who refuses apple-dumplings." (*Lamb cited Coleridge's observation that....*)

2. "The human species, according to the best theory I can form of it, is composed of two distinct races, the men who borrow, and the men who lend." (*Lamb wrote that....*)

3. "Nothing puzzles me more than time and space; and yet nothing troubles me less, as I never think about them." (*He muses that....*)

4. "When I am not walking, I am reading; I cannot sit and think." (*He admitted that....*)

5. "Sentimentally I am disposed to harmony. But organically I am incapable of a tune." (*He confesses that....*)

Exercise 47   LBCH 23a
Revising: Subjunctive mood   p. 190

Revise the following sentences with appropriate subjunctive verb forms. (The first item is answered in the back of this book.)

Example:

I would help the old man if I was able to reach him.

I would help the old man if I <u>were</u> able to reach him.

1. If John Hawkins would have known of the dangerous side effects of smoking tobacco, would he have introduced the dried plant to England in 1565?

2. Hawkins noted that if a Florida Indian was to travel for several days, he would have smoked tobacco to satisfy his hunger and thirst.

3. Early tobacco growers feared that their product would not gain acceptance unless it was perceived as healthful.

4. To prevent fires, in 1646 the General Court of Massachusetts passed a law requiring that a colonist smoked tobacco only if he was five miles from any town.

5. To prevent decadence, in 1647 Connecticut passed a law mandating that one's smoking of tobacco was limited to once a day in one's own home.

Exercise 48 √   LBCH 24
Converting between active and passive voices   p. 192

Convert the following sentences from active to passive or from passive to active. (In converting from passive to active, you may have to add a subject for the new sentence.) (An answer to the first item appears in the back of this book.)

Example:

The aspiring actor was discovered in a nightclub.

A talent scout discovered the aspiring actor in a nightclub.

                    Pasive
1. When the Eiffel Tower was built in 1889, it was thought by the French to be ugly.

        Have no meaning s
2. At that time many people still resisted industrial technology. – active

3. The tower's naked steel construction epitomized this technology. active

4. Beautiful ornament was expected to grace fine buildings.   —passive

5. Further, the tower could not even be called a building because it had — active
   no solid walls.

Exercise 49   LBCH 25
Revising: Subject-verb agreement   p. 194

Revise the verbs in the following sentences as needed to make subjects and
verbs agree in number. If the sentence is already correct as given, circle the
number preceding it. (The first item is answered in the back of this book.)

Example:

Each of the job applicants type sixty words per minute.

Each of the job applicants **types** sixty words per minute.

1. Weinstein & Associates are a consulting firm that try to make business-
   people laugh.   is   tries

2. Statistics from recent research suggests that humor relieves stress.
   They   without s

3. Reduced stress in businesses in turn reduce illness and absenteeism.
   it   + s
                                                                    it

4. Reduced stress can also reduce friction within an employee group,
   which then work together more productively.
                 s

5. In special conferences held by one consultant, each of the participants practice making the others laugh.

6. One consultant to many companies suggests cultivating office humor with practical jokes such as a rubber fish in the water cooler.

7. When employees or their manager regularly post cartoons on the bulletin board, office spirit usually picks up.

8. When someone who has seemed too easily distracted is entrusted with updating the cartoons, his or her concentration often improves.

9. In the fact of levity, the former sourpuss becomes one of those who hides bad temper.

10. Every one of the consultants caution, however, that humor has no place in life-affecting corporate situations such as employee layoffs.

PRONOUNS

Exercise 50   LBCH 26a, b
Choosing between subjective and
objective pronouns   *p. 201, 202*

From the pairs in brackets, underline the appropriate subjective or objective pronoun(s) for each of the following sentences. (The first item is answered in the back of this book.)

Example:

"Between you and [*I, me*]," the seller said, "this deal is a steal."

"Between you and <u>me</u>," the seller said, "this deal is a steal."

1. Jody and [*I, me*] had been hunting for jobs.

2. The best employees at our old company were [*she, her*] and [*I, me*], so [*we, us*] expected to find jobs quickly.

3. Between [*she, her*] and [*I, me*] the job search had lasted two months, and still it had barely begun.

4. Slowly, [*she, her*] and [*I, me*] stopped sharing leads.

5. It was obvious that Jody and [*I, me*] could not be as friendly as [*we, us*] had been.

Exercise 51   LBCH 26c
Choosing between who *and* whom   p. 202

From the pairs in brackets, underline the appropriate form of the pronoun in each of the following sentences. (The first item is answered in the back of this book.)

Example:

My mother asked me [*who, whom*] I was going out with.

My mother asked me <u>whom</u> I was going out with.

1. The school administrators suspended Jurgen, [*who, whom*] they suspected of setting the fire.

2. Jurgen had been complaining to other custodians, [who, ~~whom~~] *who* reported him. ✗

3. He constantly complained of unfair treatment from [whoever, (whomever)] happened to be passing in the halls, including pupils. ✗

4. "[Who, ~~Whom~~] *who* here has heard Mr. Jurgen's complaints?" the police asked. ✗

5. "[Who, ~~Whom~~] *whom* did he complain most about?" ✗

after from alway ~~then~~ whom and whomever

Exercise 52
Sentence combining: Who *versus* whom

LBCH 26c
p. 202

Combine each pair of sentences below into one sentence that contains a clause beginning with *who* or *whom*. Be sure to use the appropriate case form. You have to add, delete, and rearrange words. Each item may have more than one possible answer. (An answer to the first item appears in the back of this book.)

Example:

David is the candidate. We think David deserves to win.

David is the candidate <u>who</u> we think deserves to win.

1. Some children have undetected hearing problems. These children may do poorly in school.

2. They may not hear important instructions and information from teachers. Teachers may speak softly.

3. Classmates may not be audible. The teacher calls on those classmates.

4. Some hearing-impaired children may work harder to overcome their disability. These children get a lot of encouragement at home.

5. Some hearing-impaired children may take refuge in fantasy friends. They can rely on these friends not to criticize or laugh.

Exercise 53   LBCH 26d
Choosing between subjective and objective pronouns   p. 204

From the pairs in brackets, underline the appropriate subjective or objective pronoun for each of the following sentences. (The first item is answered in the back of this book.)

Example:

Convincing [we, us] veterans to vote yes will be difficult.

Convincing <u>us</u> veterans to vote yes will be difficult.

1. Obtaining enough protein is important to [we, us] vegetarians.

2. Instead of obtaining protein from meat, [we, us] vegetarians get our protein from other sources.

3. Jeff claims to know only two vegetarians, Helena and [he, him], who avoid all animal products, including milk.

4. Some of [we, us] vegetarians eat fish, which is a good source of protein.

5. [We, Us] vegetarians in my family, my parents and [I, me], drink milk
    and eat fish.

Exercise 54   LBCH 26
Revising: Case   p. 200

Revise all inappropriate case forms in the following paragraph. (The first
two sentences are answered in the back of this book.)

> Written four thousand years ago, *The Epic of*
> *Gilgamesh* tells of the friendship of Gilgamesh and Enkidu.
> Gilgamesh was a bored king who his people thought was
> too harsh. Then he met Enkidu, a wild man whom had
> lived with the animals in the mountains. Immediately,
> him and Gilgamesh wrestled to see whom was more pow-
> erful. After hours of struggle, Enkidu admitted that
> Gilgamesh was stronger than him. Now the friends need-
> ed adventures worthy of the two strongest men on earth.
> Gilgamesh said, "Between you and I, mighty deeds will be
> accomplished, and our fame will be everlasting." Among
> their acts, Enkidu and him defeated a giant bull,
> Humbaba, and cut down the bull's cedar forests. Them
> bringing back cedar logs to Gilgamesh's treeless land won
> great praise from the people. When Enkidu died,
> Gilgamesh mourned his death, realizing that no one had
> been a better friend than him. When Gilgamesh himself
> died many years later, his people raised a monument prais-
> ing Enkidu and he for their friendship and their mighty
> deeds of courage.

Exercise 55   **LBCH 27**
Revising: Pronoun-antecedent agreement   *p. 205*

Revise the following sentences so that pronouns and their antecedents agree in person and number. Some items have more than one possible answer. Try to avoid the generic *he*. If you change the subject of a sentence, be sure to change verbs as necessary for agreement. If the sentence is already correct as given, circle the number preceding it. (The first item is answered in the back of this book.)

> *Example:*
>
> Each of the Boudreau children brought their laundry home at Thanksgiving.
>
> All of the Boudreau children brought their laundry home at Thanksgiving. *Or:* Each of the Boudreau children brought laundry home at Thanksgiving. *Or:* Each of the Boudreau children brought his or her laundry home at Thanksgiving.

1. Each girl raised in a Mexican American family in the Rio Grande Valley of Texas hopes that one day they will be given a *quinceañera* party for their fifteenth birthday.

2. Such celebrations are very expensive because it entails a religious service followed by a huge party.

3. A girl's immediate family, unless they are wealthy, cannot afford the party by themselves.

4. Her parents will ask each close friend or relative if they can help with the preparations.

5. Surrounded by her family and attended by her friends and their escorts, the *quinceañera* is introduced as a young woman eligible for fashionable Mexican American society.

Exercise 56   *LBCH 28a,b*
Revising: Ambiguous and remote pronoun
reference   *pp. 209, 210*

Rewrite the following sentences to eliminate unclear pronoun reference. If you use a pronoun in your revision, be sure that it refers to only one antecedent and that it falls close enough to its antecedent to ensure clarity. (An answer to the first item appears in the back of this book.)

Example:

Saul found an old gun in the rotting shed that was just as his grandfather had left it.

In the rotting shed Saul found an old <u>gun that</u> was just as his grandfather had left it.

1. There is a difference between the heroes of the twentieth century and the heroes of earlier times: they have flaws in their characters.

2. Sports fans still admire Pete Rose, Babe Ruth, and Joe Namath even though they could not be perfect.

3. Fans liked Rose for having his young son serve as bat boy when he was in Cincinnati.

4. Rose's reputation as a gambler and tax evader may overshadow his reputation as a ball player, but it will survive.

5. Rose amassed an unequaled record as a hitter, using his bat to do things no one else has ever done. It stands even though Rose has been banned from baseball.

Exercise 57   LBCH 28c
Revising: Indefinite and inappropriate pronoun
reference   p. 211

Many of the pronouns in the following sentences do not refer to specific, appropriate antecedents. Revise the sentences as necessary to make them clear. (An answer to the first item appears in the back of this book.)

Example:

In Grand Teton National Park, they have moose, elk, and trumpeter swans.

Moose, elk, and trumpeter swans live in Grand Teton National Park.

1. "Life begins at forty" is a cliché many people live by, and this may well be true.

2. When she was forty, Pearl Buck's novel The Good Earth won the Pulitzer Prize.

3. Buck was a novelist which wrote primarily about China.

4. In The Good Earth you have to struggle, but fortitude is rewarded.

5. Buck received much critical praise and earned over $7 million, but she was very modest about it.

6. Kenneth Kaunda, past president of Zambia, was elected to it in 1964, at age forty.

7. When Catherine I became empress of Russia at age forty, they feared more than loved her.

8. At forty, Paul Revere made his famous ride to warn American revolutionary leaders that the British were going to arrest them. This gave the colonists time to prepare for battle.

9. In the British House of Commons they did not welcome forty-year-old Nancy Astor as the first female member when she entered in 1919.

10. In AD 610 Muhammad, age forty, began to have a series of visions that became the foundation of the Muslim faith. Since then, millions of people have become one.

Exercise 58   LBCH 28
Revising: Pronoun reference   *p.* 209

Revise the following paragraph so that each pronoun refers clearly to a single specific and appropriate antecedent. (An answer to the first item appears in the back of this book.)

In Charlotte Brontë's *Jane Eyre*, she is a shy young

woman that takes a job as governess. Her employer is a

rude, brooding man named Rochester. He lives in a mys-

terious mansion on the English moors, which contributes

an eerie quality to Jane's experience. Eerier still are the
fires, strange noises, and other unexplained happenings in
the house; but Rochester refuses to discuss this.
Eventually, they fall in love. On the day they are to be
married, however, she learns that he has a wife hidden in
the house. She is hopelessly insane and violent and must
be guarded at all times, which explains his strange behavior. Heartbroken, Jane leaves the moors, and many years
pass before they are reunited.

MODIFIERS

Exercise 59   **LBCH 29a,b**
Revising: Adjectives and adverbs   *pp. 213, 214*

Revise the following sentences so that adjectives and adverbs are used
appropriately. If any sentence is already correct as given, circle the number
preceding it. (The first item is answered in the back of this book.)

Example:

The announcer warned that traffic was moving very slow.

The announcer warned that traffic was moving very <u>slowly</u>.

1. King George III of England declared Samuel Johnson suitably for a
   pension.

2. Johnson was taken serious as a critic and dictionary maker.

3. Thinking about his meeting with the king, Johnson felt proudly.

4. Johnson was relieved that he had not behaved badly in the king's presence.

5. After living cheap for over twenty years, Johnson finally had enough money from the pension to eat and dress good.

Exercise 60   LBCH 29c
Revising: Comparatives and superlatives   *p. 215*

Revise the sentences below so that the comparative and superlative forms of adjectives and adverbs are appropriate for formal usage. (The first item is answered in the back of this book.)

Example:

Attending classes full-time and working at two jobs was the most impossible thing I ever did.

Attending classes full-time and working at two jobs was <u>impossible</u> [or <u>the hardest thing I ever did</u>].

1. Charlotte was the older of the three Brontë sisters, all of whom were novelists.

2. Some readers think Emily Brontë's *Wuthering Heights* is the most sad-dest novel they have ever read.

3. Of the other two sisters, Charlotte and Anne, Charlotte was probably the most talented.

4. Critics still argue about whether Charlotte or Emily wrote more better.

5. Certainly this family of women novelists was the most unique.

Exercise 61   **LBCH 29e**
Revising: Present and past participles (ESL)   *p. 217*

Revise the adjectives in the following sentences as needed to distinguish between present and past participles. If the sentence is already correct as given, circle the number preceding it. (The first item is answered in the back of this book.)

> *Example:*
>
> The subject was embarrassed to many people.
>
> The subject was <u>embarrassing</u> to many people.

1. Several critics found Alice Walker's *The Color Purple* to be a fascinated book.

2. One confused critic wished that Walker had deleted the scenes set in Africa.

3. Another critic argued that although the book contained many depressed episodes, the overall impact was excited.

4. Since other readers found the book annoyed, this critic pointed out its many surprised qualities.

5. In the end most critics agreed that the book was a satisfied novel.

Exercise 62   *LBCH 29f*
Revising: Articles (ESL)   *p. 218*

For each blank below, indicate whether *a, an, the,* or no article should be inserted. (The first item is answered in the back of this book.)

From _____ native American Indians who migrated

from _____ Asia 20,000 years ago to _____ new arrivals

who now come by _____ planes, _____ United States is

_____ nation of foreigners. It is _____ country of

immigrants who are all united under _____ single flag.

Back in _____ seventeenth and eighteenth cen-

turies, at least 75 percent of the population came from

_____ England. However, between 1820 and 1975 more

than 38 million immigrants came to this country from

elsewhere in _____ Europe. Many children of _____

immigrants were self-conscious and denied their heritage;

many even refused to learn _____ native language of

their parents and grandparents. They tried to

"Americanize" themselves. The so-called Melting Pot

theory of social change stressed _____ importance of

blending everyone together into _____ kind of stew.

Each nationality would contribute its own flavor, but

_____ final stew would be something called "American."

This Melting Pot theory was never completely successful. In the last half of this century, _____ ethnic revival has changed _____ metaphor. Many people now see _____ American society as _____ mosaic. Americans are once again proud of their heritage, and _____ ethnic differences make _____ mosaic colorful and interesting.

Exercise 63   LBCH 30a
Revising: Misplaced clauses and phrases   p. 222

Revise the following sentences so that phrases and clauses clearly modify the appropriate words. (An answer to the first item appears in the back of this book.)

Example:

I came to enjoy flying over time.

Over time I came to enjoy flying.

1. Women have contributed much to knowledge and culture of great value.

2. Emma Willard founded the Troy Female Seminary, the first institution to provide a college-level education for women in 1821.

3. Sixteen years later Mary Lyon founded Mount Holyoke Female Seminary, the first true women's college with directors and a campus who would sustain the college even after Lyon's death.

4. *Una* was the first US newspaper, which was founded by Pauline Wright Davis in 1853, that was dedicated to gaining women's rights.

5. Mitchell's Comet was discovered in 1847, which was named for Maria Mitchell.

Exercise 64   LBCH 30a
Revising: Placement of adverbs and
adjectives (ESL)   p. 223

Revise the sentences below to correct the positions of adverbs or adjectives. If a sentence is already correct as given, circle the number preceding it. (The first item is answered in the back of this book.)

Example:

Gasoline high prices affect usually car sales.

High gasoline prices usually affect car sales.

1. Some years ago Detroit cars often were praised.

2. Luxury large cars especially were prized.

3. Then a serious oil shortage led drivers to value small foreign cars that got good mileage.

4. Now with gasoline ample supplies, consumers are returning to American large cars.

5. However, the large cars not are luxury sedans but vans and sport-utility vehicles.

Exercise 65   **LBCH 30b**
Revising: Dangling modifiers   **p. 226**

Revise the following sentences to eliminate any dangling modifiers. Each item has more than one possible answer. (An answer to the first item appears in the back of this book.)

Example:

Driving north, the vegetation became increasingly sparse.

Driving north, <u>we noticed that</u> the vegetation became increasingly sparse. *Or:* <u>As we drove north</u>, the vegetation became increasingly sparse.

1. After accomplishing many deeds of valor, Andrew Jackson's fame led to his election to the Presidency in 1828 and 1832.

2. By the age of fourteen, both of Jackson's parents had died.

3. To aid the American Revolution, service as a mounted courier was chosen by Jackson.

4. Though not well educated, a successful career as a lawyer and judge proved Jackson's ability.

5. Winning many military battles, the American public believed in Jackson's leadership.

Exercise 66   **LBCH 30b**
Sentence combining: Placing modifiers   *p. 226*

Combine each pair of sentences below into a single sentence by rewriting one as a modifier. Make sure the modifier applies clearly to the appropriate word. You will have to add, delete, and rearrange words, and you may find that more than one answer is possible in each case. (An answer to the first item appears in the back of this book.)

Example:

Bob demanded a hearing from the faculty. Bob wanted to appeal the decision.

<u>Wanting to appeal the decision</u>, Bob demanded a hearing from the faculty.

1. Evening falls in the Central American rain forests. The tungara frogs begin their croaking chorus.

2. Male tungara frogs croak loudly at night. The "songs" they sing are designed to attract female frogs.

3. But predators also hear the croaking. They gather to feast on the frogs.

4. The predators are lured by their croaking dinners. The predators include bullfrogs, snakes, bats, and opossums.

5. The frogs hope to mate. Their nightly chorus can result in death instead.

Exercise 67   **LBCH 30**
Revising: Misplaced and dangling modifiers   **p. 222**

Revise the following paragraph to eliminate any misplaced or dangling modifiers. (An answer to the first item appears in the back of this book.)

> Central American tungara frogs silence several nights a week their mating croaks. When not croaking, the chance that the frogs will be eaten by predators is reduced. The frogs seem to fully believe in "safety in numbers." They more than likely will croak along with a large group rather than by themselves. By forgoing croaking on some nights, the frogs' behavior prevents the species from "croaking."

SENTENCE FAULTS

Exercise 68   **LBCH 31**
Identifying and revising sentence fragments   **p. 228**

Apply the tests for completeness to each of the following word groups. If a word group is a complete sentence, circle the number preceding it. If it is a sentence fragment, revise it in two ways: by making it a complete sentence and by combining it with a main clause written from the information given in other items. (The first two items are answered at the back of this book.)

Example:
And could not find his money.

The word group has a verb (*could . . . find*) but no subject.

Revised into a complete sentence: And *he* could not find his money.

Combined with a new main clause: *He was lost* and could not find his money.

1. In an interesting article about vandalism against works of art.

2. The motives of the vandals varying widely.

3. Those who harm artwork are usually angry.

4. But not necessarily at the artist or the owner.

5. For instance, a man who hammered at Michelangelo's *Pieta*.

6. And knocked off the Virgin Mary's nose.

7. Because he was angry at the Roman Catholic Church.

8. Which knew nothing of his grievance.

9. Although many damaged works can be repaired.

10. Usually even the most skillful repairs are forever visible.

Exercise 69   LBCH 31
Revising sentence fragments   p. 228

Correct any sentence fragment below either by combining it with a main
clause or by making it a main clause. If an item contains no sentence fragment, circle the number preceding it. (The first two items are answered at
the back of this book.)

> *Example:*
> Jujitsu is good for self-protection. Because it enables one to over-
> come an opponent without the use of weapons.
>
> Jujitsu is good for self-protection because it enables one to over-
> come an opponent without the use of weapons.

1. Human beings who perfume themselves. They are not much different
    from other animals.

2. Animals as varied as insects and dogs release *pheromones*. Chemicals
    that signal other animals.

3. Human beings have a diminished sense of smell. And do not con-
    sciously detect most of their own species' pheromones.

4. The human substitute for pheromones may be perfumes. Especially
    musk and other fragrances derived from animal oils.

5. Some sources say that humans began using perfume to cover up the
    smell of burning flesh. During sacrifices to the gods.

6. Perfumes became religious offerings in their own right. Being expensive to make, they were highly prized.

7. The earliest historical documents from the Middle East record the use of fragrances. Not only in religious ceremonies but on the body.

8. In the nineteenth century chemists began synthesizing perfume oils. Which previously could be made only from natural sources.

9. The most popular animal oil for perfume today is musk. Although some people dislike its heavy, sweet odor.

10. Synthetic musk oil would help conserve a certain species of deer. Whose gland is the source of musk.

Exercise 70   LBCH 31
Revising: Sentence fragments   *p. 228*

Revise the following paragraph to eliminate sentence fragments by combining them with main clauses or rewriting them as main clauses. (The first three sentences are answered at the back of this book.)

Baby red-eared slider turtles are brightly colored.

With bold patterns on their yellowish undershells. Which

serve as a warning to predators. The bright colors of

skunks and other animals. They signal that the animals

will spray nasty chemicals. In contrast, the turtle's colors warn largemouth bass. That the baby turtle will actively

defend itself. When a bass gulps down a turtle. The feisty

baby claws and bites. Forcing the bass to spit it out. To

avoid a similar painful experience. The bass will avoid

other baby red-eared slider turtles. The turtle loses its

bright colors as it grows too big. For a bass's afternoon

snack.

Exercise 71   **LBCH 32**
Identifying and revising comma splices   *p. 232*

Correct each comma splice below in *two* of the ways described on pages
232-235. If an item contains no comma splice, circle the number preceding
it. (The first item is answered at the back of this book.)

Example:
Carolyn still had a headache, she could not get the child-proof cap off
the aspirin bottle.

Carolyn still had a headache <u>because</u> she could not get the child-proof
cap off the aspirin bottle.

Carolyn still had a headache, <u>for</u> she could not get the child-proof cap
off the aspirin bottle.

1. Money has a long history, it goes back at least as far as the earliest
   records.

2. Many of the earliest records concern financial transactions, indeed,
   early history must often be inferred from commercial activity.

3. Every known society has had a system of money, though the objects serving as money have varied widely.

4. Sometimes the objects have had real value, in modern times, however, their value has been more abstract.

5. Cattle, fermented beverages, and rare shells have served as money, each one had actual value for the society.

Exercise 72   **LBCH 32**
Identifying and revising fused sentences   *p. 232*

Revise each of the fused sentences below in *two* ways. (An answer to the first item appears in the back of this book.)

> *Example:*
> Tim was shy he usually refused invitations.
> Tim was shy, <u>so</u> he usually refused invitations.
> Time way shy;_he usually refused invitations.

1. Throughout history money and religion were closely linked there was little distinction between government and religion.

2. The head of state and the religious leader were often the same person all power rested in one ruler.

3. These powerful leaders decided what objects would serve as money their backing encouraged public faith in the money.

4. Coins were minted of precious metals the religious overtones of money were then strengthened.

5. People already believed the precious metals to be divine their use in money intensified its allure.

Exercise 73   **LBCH 32**
Sentence combining: Comma splices and fused
  sentences   *p. 232*

Combine each pair of sentences below into one sentence without creating a comma splice or fused sentence. Combine sentences by (1) supplying a comma and coordinating conjunction, (2) supplying a semicolon, or (3) subordinating one clause to the other. You will have to add, delete, or change words as well as punctuation. (A revision of the first item appears in the back of this book.)

Example:
The sun sank lower in the sky. The colors gradually faded.

<u>As</u> the sun sank lower in the sky, the colors gradually faded. [The first clause is subordinated to the second.]

1. The exact origin of paper money is unknown. It has not survived as coins, shells, and other durable objects have.

2. Perhaps goldsmiths were also bankers. Thus they held the gold of their wealthy customers.

3. The goldsmiths probably gave customers receipts for their gold. These receipts were then used in trade.

4. The goldsmiths were something like modern-day bankers. Their receipts were something like modern-day money.

5. The goldsmiths became even more like modern-day bankers. They
    began issuing receipts for more gold than they actually held in their
    vaults.

Exercise 74   LBCH 32
Revising: Comma splices and fused sentences   *p. 232*

Identify and revise the comma splices and fused sentences in the following
paragraph. (An answer to the first sentence appears in the back of this
book.)

All those parents who urged their children to eat
broccoli were right, the vegetable really is healthful.
Broccoli contains sulforaphane, moreover, this mustard oil
can be found in kale and Brussels sprouts. Sulforaphane
causes the body to make an enzyme that attacks carcinogens, these substances cause cancer. The enzyme speeds
up the work of the kidneys then they can flush harmful
chemicals out of the body. Other vegetables have similar
benefits however, green, leafy vegetables like broccoli are
the most efficient. Thus, wise people will eat their broccoli it could extend their lives.

Exercise 75   LBCH 33
Revising: Sentences mixed in grammar or meaning   *p. 236*

Revise the following sentences so that their parts fit together both in grammar and in meaning. Each item has more than one possible answer. (An
answer to the first item appears in the back of this book.)

Example:
When they find out how expensive pianos are is why they were
discouraged.

They were discouraged <u>because</u> they found out how expensive pianos are.

When they found out how expensive pianos are, <u>they</u> were discouraged.

1. A hurricane is when the winds in a tropical depression rotate counterclockwise at more than seventy-four miles per hour.

2. Because hurricanes can destroy so many lives and so much property is why people fear them.

3. Through high winds, storm surge, floods, and tornadoes is how a hurricane can kill thousands of people.

4. Among hurricanes, they have become less deadly since 1950.

5. The reason for the lower death rates is because improved communication systems and weather satellites warn people early enough to escape the hurricane.

Exercise 76   **LBCH 33c**
Revising: Repeated sentence parts (ESL)   *p. 238*

Revise the following sentences to eliminate any unnecessary repetition of sentence parts. (An answer to the first item appears in the back of this book.)

Example:
Over 79 percent of Americans they have heard of global warming.

Over 79 percent of <u>Americans have</u> heard of global warming.

1. Global warming it is caused by the gradual erosion of the ozone layer that protects the earth from the sun.

2. Scientists who study this problem they say that the primary causes of erosion are the use of fossil fuels and the reduction of forests.

3. Many nonscientists they mistakenly believe that aerosol spray cans are the primary cause of erosion.

4. One scientist whom others respect him argues that Americans have effectively reduced their use of aerosol sprays.

5. He argues that we will stop global warming only when the public learns the real causes then.

PUNCTUATION

■

Revise the following sentences so that periods are used correctly. (The first item is answered at the back of this book.)

Example:
Several times I wrote to ask when my subscription ended?
Several times I wrote to ask when my subscription ended.

1. The instructor asked when Plato wrote *The Republic?*

2. Give the date within one century

3. The exact date is not known, but it is estimated at 370 B.C..

4. Dr Arn will lecture on Plato at 7:30 p.m..

5. The area of the lecture hall is only 1600 sq ft

Insert appropriate punctuation (periods, question marks, or exclamation points) where needed in the following paragraph. (The first sentence is answered at the back of this book.)

When visitors first arrive in Hawaii, they often encounter an unexpected language barrier Standard English is the language of business and government, but many of the people speak Pidgin English Instead of an excited "Aloha" the visitors may be greeted with an excited Pidgin "Howzit" or asked if they know "how fo' find one good hotel" Many Hawaiians question whether Pidgin will hold children back because it prevents communication with the *haoles*, or Caucasians, who run businesses Yet many others feel that Pidgin is a last defense of ethnic diversity on the islands To those who want to make standard English the official language of the state, these Hawaiians may respond, "Just 'cause I speak Pidgin no mean I dumb" They may ask, "Why you no listen" or, in standard English, "Why don't you listen"

Exercise 79   LBCH 35a
Using the comma with linked main clauses   p. 243

Insert a comma before each coordinating conjunction that links main clauses in the following sentences. (The first item is answered at the back of this book.)

Example:
I would have attended the concert and the reception but I had to baby-sit for my niece.

I would have attended the concert and the reception, but I had to baby-sit for my niece.

1. Parents once automatically gave their children the father's surname but some no longer do.

2. Instead, they bestow the mother's name for they believe that the mother's importance should be recognized.

3. The child's surname may be just the mother's or it may link the mother's and the father's with a hyphen.

4. Sometimes the first and third children will have the mother's surname and the second child will have the father's.

5. Occasionally the mother and father combine parts of their names and a new hybrid surname is born.

Exercise 80   LBCH 35b
Using the comma with introductory elements   *p. 245*

Insert commas where needed after introductory elements in the following sentences. If a sentence is punctuated correctly as given, circle the number preceding it. (The first two items are answered at the back of this book.)

Example:
After the new library opened the old one became a student union.

After the new library opened, the old one became a student union.

1. Moving in a fluid mass is typical of flocks of birds and schools of fish.

2. Because it is sudden and apparently well coordinated the movement of flocks and schools has seemed to be directed by a leader.

3. However new studies have discovered that flocks and schools are leaderless.

4. When each bird or fish senses a predator it follows individual rules for fleeing.

5. Multiplied over hundreds of individuals these responses look as if they have been choreographed.

Exercise 81   LBCH 35c
Using the comma with nonessential elements   *p. 246*

Insert commas in the following sentences to set off nonessential elements, and delete any commas that incorrectly set off essential elements. If a sentence is correct as given, circle the number preceding it. (The first item is answered at the back of this book.)

Example:
Our language has adopted the words, *garage* and *fanfare*, from the French.

Our language has adopted the words _*garage* and *fanfare* _from the French.

1. Italians insist that Marco Polo the thirteenth-century explorer did not import pasta from China.

2. Pasta which consists of flour and water and often egg existed in Italy long before Marco Polo left for his travels.

3. A historian who studied pasta places its origin in the Middle East in the fifth century.

4. Most Italians dispute this account although their evidence is shaky.

5. Wherever it originated, the Italians are now the undisputed masters, in making and cooking pasta.

6. Marcella Hazan, who has written several books on Italian cooking, insists that homemade and hand-rolled pasta is the best.

7. Most cooks must buy dried pasta lacking the time to make their own.

8. The finest pasta is made from semolina, a flour from hard durum wheat.

9. Pasta manufacturers choose hard durum wheat, because it makes firmer cooked pasta than common wheat does.

10. Pasta, made from common wheat, tends to get soggy in boiling water.

Exercise 82
Sentence combining:
Commas with nonessential elements

Combine each pair of sentences below into one sentence that uses the element described in brackets. Insert commas as appropriate. You will have to add, delete, change, and rearrange words. Some items have more than one possible answer. (An answer to the first item appears at the back of this book.)

Example:
Mr. Ward's oldest sister helped keep him alive. She was a nurse in the hospital. (*Nonessential clause beginning who.*)

Mr. Ward's oldest sister, who was a nurse in the hospital, helped keep him alive.

1. American colonists first imported pasta from the English. The English had discovered it as tourists in Italy. (*Nonessential clause beginning* <u>who</u>.)

2. The English returned from their grand tours of Italy. They were called *macaronis* because of their fancy airs. (*Nonessential phrase beginning* <u>returning</u>.)

3. A hair style was also called *macaroni*. It had elaborate curls. (*Essential phrase beginning* <u>with</u>.)

4. The song "Yankee Doodle" refers to this hairdo. It reports that Yankee Doodle "stuck a feather in his cap and called it macaroni." (*Essential clause beginning* <u>when</u>.)

5. The song was actually intended to poke fun at unrefined American colonists. It was a creation of the English. (*Nonessential appositive.*)

Exercise 83   LBCH 35d,e
Using the comma with
series and coordinate adjectives   *p. 250*

Insert commas in the following sentences to separate coordinate adjectives or elements in series. Circle the number preceding each sentence whose punctuation is already correct. (The first item is answered at the back of this book.)

Example:
Quiet by day, the club became a noisy smoky dive at night.

Quiet by day, the club became a noisy, smoky dive at night.

1. Shoes with high heels originated to protect feet from the mud garbage and animal waste in the streets.

2. The first known high heels worn strictly for fashion appeared in the sixteenth century.

3. The heels were worn by men and made of colorful silk brocades soft suedes or smooth leathers.

4. High-heeled shoes received a boost when the short powerful King Louis XIV of France began wearing them.

5. Eventually only wealthy fashionable French women wore high heels.

Exercise 84   LBCH 35f
Using the comma with dates, addresses,
place names, numbers   *p. 251*

Insert commas as needed in the following sentences. (The first item is answered at the back of this book.)

Example:
The house cost $27000 fifteen years ago.

The house cost $27,000 fifteen years ago.

1. The festival will hold a benefit dinner and performance on March 10 2002 in Asheville.

2. The organizers hope to raise more than $100000 from donations and ticket sales.

3. Performers are expected from as far away as Milan Italy and Kyoto Japan.

4. All inquiries sent to Mozart Festival PO Box 725 Asheville North Carolina 28803 will receive a quick response.

5. The deadline for ordering tickets by mail is Monday December 3 2001.

Exercise 85   LBCH 35g
Using the comma or semicolon with quotations   p. 252

Insert commas or semicolons in the following sentences to correct punctuation with quotations. Circle the number preceding any sentence whose punctuation is already correct. (The first two items are answered at the back of this book.)

Example:
The shoplifter declared "I didn't steal anything."

The shoplifter declared, "I didn't steal anything."

1. The writer and writing teacher Peter Elbow proposes an "open-ended writing process that can change you, not just your words."

2. "I think of the open-ended writing process as a voyage in two stages" Elbow says.

3. "The sea voyage is a process of divergence, branching, proliferation, and confusion" Elbow continues "the coming to land is a process of convergence, pruning, centralizing, and clarifying."

4. "Keep up one session of writing long enough to get loosened up and tired" advises Elbow "long enough in fact to make a bit of a voyage."

5. "In coming to new land" Elbow says "you develop a new conception of what you are writing about."

Exercise 86   **LBCH 35h**
Revising: Needless or misused commas   *p. 253*

Revise the following sentences to eliminate needless or misused commas.
Circle the number preceding each sentence that is already punctuated correctly. (The first item is answered at the back of this book.)

Example:
The portrait of the founder, that hung in the dining hall, was stolen by
pranksters.

The portrait of the founder_that hung in the dining hall_was stolen by
pranksters.

1. Nearly 32 million US residents, speak a first language other than
   English.

2. After English the languages most commonly spoken in the United
   States are, Spanish, French, and German.

3. Almost 75 percent of the people, who speak foreign languages, used the
   words, "good' or "very good," when judging their proficiency in English.

4. Recent immigrants, especially those speaking Spanish, Chinese, and
   Korean, tended to judge their English more harshly.

5. The states with the highest proportion of foreign language speakers, are
   New Mexico, and California.

Exercise 87   **LBCH 35**
Revising: Commas   *p. 243*

Insert commas in the following paragraphs wherever they are needed, and
eliminate any misused or needless commas. (The first sentence is answered
at the back of this book.)

Ellis Island New York has reopened for business but

now the customers are tourists not immigrants. This spot

which lies in New York Harbor was the first American soil seen, or touched by many of the nation's immigrants. Though other places also served as ports of entry for foreigners none has the symbolic power of, Ellis Island. Between its opening in 1892 and its closing in 1954, over 20 million people about two-thirds of all immigrants were detained there before taking up their new lives in the United States. Ellis Island processed over 2000 newcomers a day when immigration was at its peak between 1900 and 1920.

As the end of a long voyage and the introduction to the New World Ellis Island must have left something to be desired. The "huddled masses" as the Statue of Liberty calls them indeed were huddled. New arrivals were herded about kept standing in lines for hours or days yelled at and abused. Assigned numbers they submitted their bodies to the pokings and proddings of the silent nurses and doctors, who were charged with ferreting out the slightest sign of sickness, disability or insanity. That test having been passed the immigrants faced interrogation by an official through an interpreter. Those, with names deemed inconveniently long or difficult to pronounce, often found

themselves permanently labeled with abbreviations, of

their names, or with names, of their hometowns. But,

millions survived the examination humiliation and confu-

sion, to take the last short boat ride to New York City.

For many of them and especially for their descendants

Ellis Island eventually became not a nightmare but the

place where life began.

Exercise 88   **LBCH 36b**
Using the semicolon between main clauses   *p. 256*

Insert a semicolon in each sentence below to separate main clauses related
by a conjunctive adverb or transitional expression, and insert a comma or
commas where needed to set off the adverb or expression. (The first item is
answered at the back of this book.)

Example:
He knew that tickets for the concert would be scarce therefore he
arrived at the box office hours before it opened.

He knew that tickets for the concert would be scarce; therefore, he
arrived at the box office hours before it opened.

1. Music is a form of communication like language the basic elements
   however are not letters but notes.

2. Computers can process any information that can be represented numer-
   ically as a result they can process musical information.

3. A computer's ability to process music depends on what software it can
   run it must moreover be connected to a system that converts electrical
   vibration into sound.

4. Computers and their sound systems can produce many different sounds indeed the number of possible sounds is infinite.

5. The powerful music computers are very expensive therefore they are used only by professional musicians.

Exercise 89   LBCH 36d
Revising: Misused or overused semicolons   p. 257

Revise the following sentences to eliminate misused or overused semi-colons, substituting other punctuation as appropriate. (The first item is answered at the back of this book.)

Example:
The doctor gave everyone the same advice; get exercise.
The doctor gave everyone the same advice: get exercise.

1. The main religion in India is Hinduism; a way of life as well as a theology and philosophy.

2. Unlike Christianity and Judaism; Hinduism is a polytheistic religion; with deities numbering in the hundreds.

3. Hinduism is unlike many other religions; it allows its creeds and practices to vary widely from place to place and person to person. Other religions have churches; Hinduism does not. Other religions have principal prophets and holy books; Hinduism does not. Other religions have specially trained priests or other leaders; Hinduism promotes the individual as his or her own priest.

4. In Hindu belief there are four types of people; reflective, emotional, active, and experimental.

5. Each type of person has a different technique for realizing the true, immortal self; which has infinite existence, infinite knowledge, and infinite joy.

Exercise 90
Revising: Semicolons

Insert semicolons in the following paragraph wherever they are needed.
Eliminate any misused or needless semicolons, substituting other punctuation as appropriate. (a revision of the first two sentences appears at the
back of this book.)

The set, sounds, and actors in the movie captured the

essence of horror films. The set was ideal; dark, deserted

streets, trees dipping their branches over the sidewalks,

mist hugging the ground and creeping up to meet the

trees, looming shadows of unlighted, turreted houses. The

sounds, too, were appropriate, especially terrifying was the

hard, hollow sound of footsteps echoing throughout the

film. But the best feature of the movie was its actors; all

of them tall, pale, and thin to the point of emaciation.

With one exception, they were dressed uniformly in gray

and had gray hair. The exception was an actress who

dressed only in black; as if to set off her pale yellow, near-

ly white, long hair; the only color in the film. The glint-

ing black eyes of another actor stole almost every scene,

indeed, they were the source of all the film's mischief.

Exercise 91   **LBCH 37**
Revising: Colons   *p. 258*

Insert colons as needed in the following sentences, or delete colons that are
misused. (The first item is answered at the back of this book.)

Example:
Mix the ingredients as follows sift the flour and salt together, add the
milk, and slowly beat in the egg yolk.

Mix the ingredients as follows: sift the flour and salt together, add the
milk, and slowly beat in the egg yolk.

1. In the remote parts of many Third World countries, simple signs mark
    human habitation a dirt path, a few huts, smoke from a campfire.

2. In the built-up sections of industrialized countries, nature is all but
    obliterated by signs of human life, such as: houses, factories, skyscrap-
    ers, and highways.

3. The spectacle makes many question the words of Ecclesiastes 1.4 "One
    generation passeth away, and another cometh; but the earth abideth
    forever."

4. Yet many scientists see the future differently they hold that human
    beings have all the technology necessary to clean up the earth and
    restore the cycles of nature.

5. All that is needed is: a change in the attitudes of those who use tech-
    nology.

Exercise 92   **LBCH 38a**
Forming possessives with the apostrophe   **p. 260**

Form the possessive case of each word or word group in brackets. (The first sentence is answered at the back of this book.)

Example:
The [*men*] blood pressures were higher than the [*women*].

The <u>men's</u> blood pressures were higher than the <u>women's</u>.

1. In the myths of the ancient Greeks, the [*goddesses*] roles vary widely.

2. [*Demeter*] responsibility is the fruitfulness of the earth.

3. [*Artemis*] function is to care for wild animals and small children.

4. [*Athena and Artemis*] father, Zeus, is the king of the gods.

5. Athena is concerned with fertility and with [*children*] well-being, since [*Athens*] strength depended on a large and healthy population.

Exercise 93   **LBCH 38d**
Using the apostrophe with some plurals   **p. 263**

Form the plural of each item below by adding -s, by using or not using an apostrophe (as appropriate), and by underlining or italicizing appropriately. (The first item is answered at the back of this book.)

1. 7   4. and
2. q   5. SOS
3. if

Exercise 94   **LBCH 38**
Revising: Apostrophes   *p. 260*

In the following paragraph correct any mistakes in the use of the apostrophe or any confusion between contractions and possessive personal pronouns. (The first sentence is answered at the back of this book.)

Landlocked Chad is among the worlds most troubled countries. The people's of Chad are poor: they're average per capita income equals $600 a year. Just over 40 percent of Chads population is literate, and every five hundred people must share only two teacher's. The natural resources of the nation have never been plentiful, and now, as it's slowly being absorbed into the growing Sahara Desert, even water is scarce. Chads political conflicts go back before the twentieth century, when the French colonized the land by brutally subduing it's people. The rule of the French—who's inept government of the colony did nothing to ease tensions among racial, tribal, and religious group's—ended with independence in 1960. But since then the Chadians experience has been one of civil war and oppression, and their also threatened with invasions from they're neighbors.

Exercise 95   **LBCH 39**
Revising: Quotation marks   *p. 264*

Insert quotation marks as needed in the following paragraph. (The first sentence is answered at the back of this book.)

In one class we talked about a passage from I Have a Dream, the speech delivered by Martin Luther King, Jr., on the steps of the Lincoln Memorial on August 28, 1963:

> When the architects of our republic wrote the magnificent words of the Constitution and the Declaration of Independence, they were signing a promissory note to which every American was to fall heir. This note was a promise that all men would be guaranteed the unalienable rights of life, liberty, and the pursuit of happiness.

What did Dr. King mean by this statement? the teacher asked. Perhaps we should define promissory note first. Then she explained that a person who signs such a note agrees to pay a specific sum of money on a particular date or on demand by the holder of the note. One student suggested, Maybe Dr. King meant that those who wrote and signed the Constitution and Declaration had stated the country's promise that all people in America should have equal political rights and equal opportunity for the pursuit of happiness. He and over 200,000 people had gathered in Washington, DC, added another student. Maybe their purpose was to demand payment, to demand those rights for African Americans. The whole discussion was an eye opener for those of us (including me) who had never considered that those documents make promises that we should expect our country to fulfill.

Exercise 96   **LBCH 34-40**
Revising: Punctuation   *pp. 241-274*

The following paragraphs are unpunctuated except for end-of-sentence periods. Insert periods, commas, semicolons, apostrophes, quotation marks, colons, dashes, or brackets where they are required. When different marks would be appropriate in the same place, be able to defend the choice you make. (The first two sentences are answered at the back of this book.)

Brewed coffee is the most widely consumed beverage in the world. The trade in coffee beans alone amounts to well over $6000000000 a year and the total volume of beans traded exceeds 4250000 tons a year. Its believed that the beverage was introduced into Arabia in the fifteenth century AD probably by Ethiopians. By the middle or late sixteenth century the Arabs had introduced the beverage to the Europeans who at first resisted it because of its strong flavor and effect as a mild stimulant. The French Italians and other Europeans incorporated coffee into their diets by the seventeenth century the English however preferred tea which they were then importing from India. Since America was colonized primarily by the English Americans also preferred tea. Only after the Boston Tea Party 1773 did Americans begin drinking coffee in large quantities. Now though the US is one of the top coffee-consuming countries consumption having been spurred on by familiar advertising claims Good till the last drop Rich hearty aroma Always rich never bitter.

Produced from the fruit of an evergreen tree coffee is grown primarily in Latin America southern Asia and Africa. Coffee trees require a hot climate high humidity rich soil with good drainage and partial shade consequently they thrive on the east or west slopes of tropical volcanic mountains where the soil is laced with potash and drains easily. The coffee beans actually seeds grow inside bright red berries. The berries are picked by hand and the beans are extracted by machine leaving a pulpy fruit residue that can be used for fertilizer. The beans are usually roasted in ovens a chemical process that releases the beans essential oil caffeol which gives coffee its distinctive aroma. Over a hundred different varieties of beans are produced in the world each with a different flavor attributable to three factors the species of plant *Coffea arabica* and *Coffea robusta* are the most common and the soil and climate where the variety was grown.

SPELLING
AND MECHANICS

■

Apply spelling conventions according to the instructions below. Consult a dictionary as needed. (The first item of each group is answered at the back of this book.)

a. Insert *ie* or *ei*:

1. br____f	5. for____gn	9. l____surely
2. dec____ve	6. pr____st	10. ach____ve
3. rec____pt	7. gr____vance	11. pat____nce
4. s____ze	8. f____nd	12. p____rce

b. Combine the following words and endings, keeping or dropping the final *e*'s:

1. malice + ious	4. retire + ment	7. note + able
2. love + able	5. sue + ing	8. battle + ing
3. service +able	6. virtue + ous	9. suspense + ion

c. Combine the following words and endings, changing or keeping the final *y*'s:

1. imply + s   4. delay + ing   7. solidify + s

2. messy + er   5. defy + ance   8. Murphy + s

3. apply + ing   6. say + s   9. supply + ed

d. Combine the following words and endings, doubling final consonants
    as necessary:

1. repair + ing   4. shop + ed   7. drip + ing

2. admit + ance   5. conceal + ed   8. declaim + ed

3. benefit + ed   6. allot + ed   9. parallel + ing

e. Make correct plurals of the following singular words:

1. pile   7. switch   12. video

2. donkey   8. sister-in-law   13. thief

3. beach   9. Bales   14. goose

4. summary   10. cupful   15. hiss

5. mile per hour   11. libretto   16. appendix

6. box

Exercise 98   LBCH 42a
Using hyphens in compound words   p. 281

Insert hyphens as needed in the following compounds. Circle all compounds that are correct as given. Consult a dictionary as needed. (The first
two items are answered at the back of this book.)

1. reimburse

2. deescalate

3. forty odd soldiers

4. little known bar

5. seven eighths

6. seventy eight

7. happy go lucky

8. preexisting

9. senator elect

10. postwar

11. two and six person cars

12. ex songwriter

13. V shaped

14. reeducate

Exercise 99
Revising: Capitals

LBCH 43
p. 283

Capitalize words as necessary in the following sentences, or substitute small letters for unnecessary capitals. Consult a dictionary if you are in doubt. If the capitalization in a sentence is already correct, circle the number preceding the sentence. (The first item is answered at the back of this book.)

Example:
The first book on the reading list is mark twain's *a connecticut yankee in king arthur's court.*

The first book on the reading list is Mark Twain's *A Connecticut Yankee in King Arthur's Court.*

1.   San Antonio, texas, is a thriving city in the Southwest.

2.   The city has always offered much to tourists interested in the roots of spanish settlement of the new world.

3.   The alamo is one of five Catholic Missions built by Priests to convert native americans and to maintain spain's claims in the area.

4. But the alamo is more famous for being the site of an 1836 battle that helped to create the republic of Texas.

5. Many of the nearby Streets, such as Crockett street, are named for men who gave their lives in that Battle.

6. The Hemisfair plaza and the San Antonio river link new tourist and convention facilities developed during mayor Cisneros's terms.

7. Restaurants, Hotels, and shops line the River. The haunting melodies of "Una paloma blanca" and "malagueña" lure passing tourists into Casa rio and other excellent mexican restaurants.

8. The university of Texas at San Antonio has expanded, and a Medical Center has been developed in the Northwest part of the city.

9. Sea World, on the west side of San Antonio, entertains grandparents, fathers and mothers, and children with the antics of dolphins and seals.

10. The City has attracted high-tech industry, creating a corridor of economic growth between san antonio and austin and contributing to the texas economy.

Exercise 100   **LBCH 44**
Revising: Underlining or italics   *p. 287*

Underline or italicize words and phrases as needed in the following sentences, or circle any words or phrases that are underlined unnecessarily.

Note that some highlighting is correct as given. (The first item is answered at the back of this book.)

Example:
Of Hitchcock's movies, Psycho is the scariest.

Of Hitchcock's movies, <u>Psycho</u> is the scariest.

1. Of the many Vietnam veterans who are writers, Oliver Stone is perhaps the most famous for writing and directing the films Platoon and Born on the Fourth of July.

2. Tim O'Brien has written short stories for Esquire, GQ, and Massachusetts Review.

3. Going After Cacciato is O'Brien's dreamlike novel about the horrors of combat.

4. The word Vietnam is technically two words (<u>Viet</u> and <u>Nam</u>), but most American writers spell it as <u>one</u> word.

5. American writers use words or phrases borrowed from the Vietnamese language, such as di di mau ("go quickly") or dinky dau ("crazy").

6. Philip Caputo's <u>gripping</u> account of his service in Vietnam appears in the book A Rumor of War.

7. Caputo's book was made into a television movie, also titled <u>A Rumor of War</u>.

8. David Rabe's plays—including The Basic Training of Pavlo Hummel, Streamers, and Sticks and Bones—depict the effects of the war <u>not only</u> on the soldiers <u>but</u> on their families.

9. Called the <u>poet laureate of the Vietnam war</u>, Steve Mason has published two collections of poems: Johnny's Song and Warrior for Peace.

10. The Washington Post published <u>rave</u> reviews of Veteran's Day, an autobiography by Rod Kane.

Exercise 101   **LBCH 45**
Revising: Abbreviations   *p. 290*

Revise the following sentences as needed to correct inappropriate use of abbreviations for nontechnical writing. Circle the number preceding any sentences in which the abbreviations are already appropriate as written. (The first item is answered at the back of this book.)

> *Example:*
> One prof. lectured for five hrs.
> One <u>professor</u> lectured for five <u>hours</u>.

1. In the Sept. 17, 1993, issue of *Science* magazine, Virgil L. Sharpton discusses a theory that could help explain the extinction of dinosaurs.

2. About 65 mill. yrs. ago, a comet or asteroid crashed into the earth.

3. The result was a huge crater about 10 km. (6.2 mi.) deep in the Gulf of Mex.

4. Sharpton's new measurements suggest that the crater is 50 pct. larger than scientists previously believed.

5. Indeed, 20-yr.-old drilling cores reveal that the crater is about 186 mi. wide, roughly the size of Conn.

6. The space object was traveling more than 100,000 miles per hour and hit earth with the impact of 100 to 300 million megatons of TNT.

7. On impact, 200,000 cubic km. of rock and soil were vaporized or thrown into the air.

8. That's the equivalent of 2.34 bill. cubic ft. of matter.

9. The impact would have created 400-ft. tidal waves across the Atl. Ocean, temps. higher than 20,000 degs., and powerful earthquakes.

10. Sharpton theorizes that the dust, vapor, and smoke from this impact blocked the sun's rays for mos., cooled the earth, and thus resulted in the death of the dinosaurs.

Exercise 102   **LBCH 46**
Revising: Numbers   *p. 292*

Revise the following sentences so that numbers are used appropriately for nontechnical writing. Circle the number preceding any sentence in which numbers are already used appropriately. (The first item is answered at the back of this book.)

Example:
Carol paid two hundred five dollars for used scuba gear.

Carol paid $205 for used scuba gear.

1. The planet Saturn is nine hundred million miles, or nearly ten billion five hundred million kilometers, from Earth.

2. Saturn revolves around the sun much more slowly than Earth does: a year on Saturn equals almost thirty of our years.

3. Thus, Saturn orbits the sun only two and four-tenths times during the average human life span.

4. It travels in its orbit at about twenty-one thousand six hundred miles per hour.

5. 15 to 20 times denser than Earth's core, Saturn's core measures 17,000 miles across.

6. The temperature at Saturn's cloud tops is minus one hundred seventy degrees Fahrenheit.

7. In nineteen hundred thirty-three, astronomers found on Saturn's surface a huge white spot 2 times the size of Earth and 7 times the size of Mercury.

8. Saturn's famous rings reflect almost 70 percent of the sunlight that approaches the planet.

9. The ring system is almost forty thousand miles wide, beginning 8,800 miles from the planet's visible surface and ending forty-seven thousand miles from that surface.

10. Saturn generates about one hundred thirty trillion kilowatts of electricity.

RESEARCH
AND DOCUMENTATION
■

Exercise 103   **LBCH 49a-b**
Evaluating and synthesizing sources   **p. 325-330**

The three passages below address the same issue, the legalization of drugs.
What similarities do you see in the author's ideas? What differences? Write
a paragraph of your own in which you use these authors' views as a point of
departure for your own view about drug legalization. (A sample analysis of
the similarities and differences appears at the end of this book.)

> Perhaps the most unfortunate victims of drug prohibi-
> tion laws have been the residents of America's ghettos.
> These laws have proved largely futile in deterring ghetto-
> dwellers from becoming drug abusers, but they do account
> for much of what ghetto residents identify as the drug
> problem. Aggressive, gun-toting drug dealers often upset
> law-abiding residents far more than do addicts nodding
> out in doorways. Meanwhile other residents perceive the
> drug dealers as heroes and successful role models. They're
> symbols of success to children who see no other options.
> At the same time the increasingly harsh criminal penal-
> ties imposed on adult drug dealers have led drug traffickers
> to recruit juveniles. Where once children started dealing
> drugs only after they had been using them for a few years,
> today the sequence is often reversed. Many children start
> using drugs only after working for older drug dealers for a
> while. Legalization of drugs, like legalization of alcohol in
> the early 1930s, would drive the drug-dealing business off
> the streets and out of apartment buildings and into gov-
> ernment-regulated, tax-paying stores. It also would force
> many of the gun-toting dealers out of the business and
> convert others into legitimate businessmen.
> —ETHAN A. NADELMANN, "Shooting Up"

Statistics argue against legalization. The University of Michigan conducts an annual survey of twelfth graders, asking the students about their drug consumption. In 1980, 60 percent of those polled said they had used marijuana in the past twelve months, whereas in 1996 only 44 percent had done so. Cocaine use was halved in the same period (15 percent of 7 percent). At the same time, twelve-month use of legally available drugs – alcohol and nicotine-containing cigarettes – remained constant at about 80 percent and 68 percent, respectively. The numbers of illegal drug users haven't declined nearly enough: those teenaged marijuana and cocaine users are still vulnerable to addiction and even death, and they threaten to infect their impressionable peers. But clearly the prohibition of illegal drugs has helped, while the legal status of alcohol and cigarettes has not made them less popular.

–SYLVIA RUNKLE, "The Case Against Legalization"

I have to laugh at the debate over what to do about the drug problem. Everyone is running around offering solutions – from making drug use a more serious criminal offense to legalizing it. But there isn't a real solution. I know that. I used and abused drugs, and people, and society, for two decades. Nothing worked to get me to stop all that behavior except just plain being sick and tired. Nothing. Not threats, not ten-plus years in prison, not anything that was said to me. I used until I got through. Period. And that's when you'll win the war. When all the dope fiends are done. Not a minute before.

–MICHAEL W. POSEY, "I Did Drugs Until
They Wore Me Out. Then I Stopped."

Exercise 104   LBCH 49c
Summarizing and paraphrasing   *p. 330*

Prepare two source notes, one containing a summary of the entire paragraph below and the other containing a paraphrase of the first four sentences (ending with the word *autonomy*). (A possible summary appears at the back of this book.)

Federal organization [of the United States] has made it possible for the different states to deal with the same problems in many different ways. One consequence of federalism, then, has been that people are treated differently, by law, from state to state. The great strength of this system is that differences from state to state in cultural preferences, moral standards, and levels of wealth can be accommodated. In contrast to a unitary system in which the central government makes all important decisions (as in France), federalism is a powerful arrangement for maximizing regional freedom and autonomy. The great weakness of our federal system, however, is that people in some states receive less than the best or the most advanced or the least expensive services and policies that government can offer. The federal dilemma does not invite easy solutions, for the costs and benefits of the arrangement have tended to balance out.

—Peter E. Eisinger et al., *American Politics*, p. 44

Exercise 105   **LBCH 49c**
Combining summary, paraphrase,
and direct quotation   *p. 330*

Prepare a source note containing a combination of paraphrase or summary and direct quotation that states the major idea of the passage below. (A possible answer for the first sentence appears at the back of this book.)

Most speakers unconsciously duel even during seemingly casual conversations, as can often be observed at social gatherings where they show less concern for exchanging information with other guests than for asserting their own dominance. Their verbal dueling often employs very subtle weapons like mumbling, a hostile act which defeats the listener's desire to understand what the speaker claims he is trying to say (but is really not saying because he is mumbling!). Or the verbal dueler may keep talking after someone has passed out of hearing range— which is often an aggressive challenge to the listener to return and acknowledge the dominance of the speaker.

—Peter K. Farb, *Word Play*, p. 107

Exercise 106   **LBCH 49d**
Recognizing plagiarism   *p. 334*

The numbered items below show various attempts to quote or paraphrase the following passage. Carefully compare each attempt with the original passage. On the blank line after each passage, note whether it is acceptable or not. If not, note whether it is plagiarized, inaccurate, or both, and why. (The first item is answered at the back of this book.)

I would agree with the sociologists that psychiatric labeling is dangerous. Society can inflict terrible wounds by discrimination, and by confusing health with disease and disease with badness.
                              –George E. Vaillant, *Adaptation to Life*, p. 361

1. According to George Vaillant, society often inflicts wounds by using psychiatric labeling, confusing health, disease, and badness (361).

   _____plogiarism___wo___quotes____
   ___phorephorored_____

2. According to George Vaillant, "psychiatric labeling [such as 'homosexual' or 'schizophrenic'] is dangerous. Society can inflict terrible wounds by . . . confusing health with disease and disease with badness" (361).

   ___incorect_____

3. According to George Vaillant, when psychiatric labeling discriminates between health and disease or between disease and badness, it can inflict wounds on those labeled (361).

   ___acceptable_____

4. Psychiatric labels can badly hurt those labeled, says George
    Vaillant, because they fail to distinguish among health, illness, and
    immorality (361).

    inaccurate

5. Labels such as "homosexual" and "schizophrenic" can be hurtful
    when they fail to distinguish among health, illness, and immorality.
    you need (Vaillant, 361).
    ~~correct~~ ~~incorrect~~
    incorrect — phrasephrased
    Oral interpretation

6. "I would agree with the sociologists that society can inflict terrible
    wounds by discrimination, and by confusing health with disease
    and disease with badness" (Vaillant 361).

    miss quoting him.
    incorrect.

Exercise 107   **LBCH 49e**
Integrating sources   *p. 339*

Drawing on the ideas in the following paragraph and using examples from
your own observations and experiences, write a paragraph about anxiety.
Integrate at least one direct quotation and one paraphrase from the following paragraph into your own sentences. In your paragraph identify the
author by name and give his credentials: he is a professor of psychiatry and
a practicing psychoanalyst.

> There are so many ways in which man is different
> from all the lower forms of animals, and almost all of
> them make us uniquely susceptible to feelings of anxious-
> ness. Our imagination and reasoning powers facilitate
> anxiety; the anxious feeling is precipitated not by an
> absolute impending threat—such as the worry about an
> examination, a speech, travel—but rather by the symbolic

and often unconscious representations. We do not have
to be experiencing a potential danger. We can experience
something related to it. We can recall, through our
incredible memories, the original symbolic sense of vul-
nerability in childhood and suffer the feeling attached to
that. We can even forget the original memory and still be
stuck with the emotion—which is then compounded by
its seemingly irrational quality at this time. It is not just
the fear of death which pains us, but the anticipation of
it; or the anniversary of a specific death; or a street, a hospital, a time of day, a color, a flower, a symbol associated
with death.

—Willard Gaylin, "Feeling Anxious," p. 23

Exercise 108   **LBCH 51b**
Writing MLA works-cited entries   *p. 357*

Prepare MLA works-cited entries from the information below, following the
models of the *MLA Handbook* given in 51b. (The first item is answered at
the back of this book.)

1. An article titled "Credit and Consumer Confidence" by Jocelyn Kim.
   The article appears in volume 12, issue 4, of *Adaptation to Change*, a
   journal that pages issues separately. Volume 12 is dated 1998. The
   article runs from page 101 to page 106.

   Kim, Jocelyn, "Credit and Consumer Confidence."
   Adaptation to Change × 12.4(1998): 101–106.

2. A book called *Black Voices: An Anthology of Afro-American Literature*,
   published in 1968 by the New American Library in New York, edited
   by Abraham Clapham.

   Clapham, Abraham, ed. *Black Voice: An Antology of
   Afro-American Literature*. New York: New Amer
   Library, 1968.

3. An article you consulted on March 12, 1997, over the Internet. The
   article is titled "The Meaning of *The Funeral Elegy*" and is by Jane
   Downing, Bruce Newell, and Achibo Lauro. It appears in the online
   journal *Shakespeare*, volume 4, issue 1, published in 1996. The article is

   Anderson, John Q. "The New Orleans Voodoo Ritual
   Dance and it's Twentieth Century Survival."
   Southern Folklore Quarterly 24(1960): 135–14

thirty-seven paragraphs long. The address for the article is http://www.shakespeare-cambridge.com/downing.html.

4. An article in *Southern Folklore Quarterly*, volume 24, published in 1960. The article is "The New Orleans Voodoo Ritual Dance and Its Twentieth-Century Survivals," written by John Q. Anderson, on pages 135 through 143. The journal is paged continuously throughout the annual volume.

5. An article on CD-ROM that is also available in print. The author is Susan Chu. The title is "1996 Election Returns May Widen Gender Gap." The article appears in the January 1997 issue of *Politics and Values*, a monthly magazine, on pages 12 through 26. It also appears on the CD-ROM titled *Resource/One*, released in March 1997 by UMI-ProQuest.

SAMPLE ANSWERS

Exercise 7   Revising: Emphasis of subjects and verbs, p. 5

Possible answers:

1. <u>Many heroes helped</u> to emancipate the slaves.

2. <u>Harriet Tubman,</u> an escaped slave herself, guided hundreds of other slaves to freedom on the Underground Railroad.

Exercise 8   Sentence combining: Beginnings and endings, p. 6

Possible answers:

1. <u>Pat Taylor strode into the packed room,</u> greeting students called "Taylor's Kids" and nodding to their parents and teachers.

2. <u>This wealthy Louisiana oilman had promised his "Kids" free college educations</u> because he was determined to make higher education available to all qualified but disadvantaged students.

Exercise 9   Sentence combining: Coordination, p. 7

Possible revision:

1. Many chronic misspellers do not have the time <u>or</u> motivation to master spelling rules. They may rely on dictionaries to catch misspellings, <u>but</u> most dictionaries list words under their correct spellings. One kind of dictionary is designed for chronic misspellers. It lists each word under its common *misspellings* <u>and</u> then provides the correct spelling and definition.

Exercise 10   Sentence combining: Subordination, p. 7

Possible answers:

1. When the bombardier beetle sees an enemy, it shoots out a jet of
    chemicals to protect itself.
    Seeing an enemy, the bombardier beetle shoots out a jet of chemicals
    to protect itself.
2. Consisting of hot and irritating chemicals, the beetle's spray is very
    potent.
    The beetle's spray of hot and irritating chemicals is very potent.

Exercise 11   Revising: Coordination and subordination, p. 9

Possible revision:

    Sir Walter Raleigh personified the Elizabethan Age, the period during
which Elizabeth I ruled England, in the last half of the sixteenth century.

Exercise 12   Sentence combining: Parallelism, p. 9

Possible answer:

1. People can develop post-traumatic stress disorder (PTSD) after experi-
    encing a dangerous situation and fearing for their survival.

Exercise 13   Revising: Parallelism, p. 11

Possible revision:

    The great white shark has an undeserved bad reputation. Many people
consider the great white not only swift and powerful but also a cunning and
cruel predator on humans.

Exercise 14   **Revising: Variety, p. 11**

Possible revision:

<u>After being</u> dormant for many year<u>s, t</u>he Italian volcano Vesuvius exploded on August 24 in the year AD 79.

Exercise 15   **Revising: Appropriate words, p. 12**

Possible answers:

1. Acquired immune deficiency syndrome (AIDS) is a <u>serious threat</u> all over the world.
2. The disease <u>is transmitted</u> primarily by sexual intercourse, exchange of bodily fluids, shared needles, and blood transfusions.
3. Those who think the disease is limited to <u>homosexuals</u> and <u>drug users</u> are quite mistaken.

Exercise 16   **Revising: Denotation, p. 14**

1. Maxine Hong Kingston was <u>awarded</u> many prizes for her first two books, *The Woman Warrior* and *China Men.*

Exercise 17   **Considering the connotations of words, p. 15**

1. AIDS is a serious health <u>problem.</u>

Exercise 18   **Revising: Concrete and specific words, p. 16**

Possible revision:

I remember <u>as if it were last week</u> how <u>frightened</u> I felt the first time I <u>neared</u> Mrs. Murphy's second-grade class.

Exercise 19   Using prepositions in idioms, p. 16

1. As Mark and Lana waited <u>for</u> the justice of the peace, they seemed oblivious <u>to</u> [or <u>of</u>] the other people in the lobby.

Exercise 20   Revising: Trite expressions, p. 17

Possible answers:

1. The <u>disasters</u> of the war have shaken the small nation <u>severely</u>.

Exercise 21   Revising: Subjects and verbs; empty words and phrases, p. 18

Possible answer:

1. *Gerrymandering* <u>means redrawing</u> the lines of a voting district to benefit a particular party or ethnic group.

Exercise 22   Revising: Unnecessary repetition, p. 19

Possible answer:

1. <u>After their tours of duty</u>, some Vietnam veterans had problems <u>readjusting to</u> life in America.

Exercise 23   Revising: Conciseness, p. 20

Possible answer:

1. <u>The Mexican general Antonio López de Santa Anna introduced</u> chewing gum to the United States.

Exercise 24   **Revising: Conciseness, p. 21**

Possible answer:

<u>After much thought</u>, he <u>concluded</u> that the situation with carcinogens <u>could be treated like automobiles</u>.

Exercise 25   **Identifying nouns, verbs, and pronouns, p. 23**

      N   V
1. The <u>trees</u> <u>died</u>.

Exercise 26   **Using nouns and verbs, p. 23**

Possible answer:

1. Blow out the candles and make a <u>wish</u>. [Noun.] The child <u>wished</u> for a new bicycle. [Verb.]

Exercise 27   **Identifying adjectives and adverbs, p. 25**

      adj   adj
1. The <u>icy</u> rain created <u>glassy</u> patches on the roads.

Exercise 28   **Sentence combining: Prepositional phrases, p. 25**

Possible answer:

1. The slow loris of Southeast Asia protects itself well with a poisonous chemical.

Exercise 29   **Identifying subjects and predicates, p. 26**

      subject predicate
1. The leaves I fell.

Exercise 30   **Identifying sentence patterns, p. 26**

$$\text{DO} \qquad \text{OC}$$
1. Many people find <u>New Orleans</u> <u>exciting</u>.
   Verb: <u>Find</u> is transitive

Exercise 31   **Identifying verbals and verbal phrases, p. 27**

1. <u>Written in 1850 by Nathaniel Hawthorne,</u> *The Scarlet Letter* tells the
   story of Hester Prynne.
   (adjective)

Exercise 32   **Sentence combining: Verbals and verbal phrases, p. 28**

Possible answer:

1. Air pollution is a health problem <u>affecting millions of Americans.</u>

Exercise 33   **Identifying subordinate clauses, p. 29**

1. Scientists<u> who want to catch the slightest signals from space</u> use
   extremely sensitive receivers.
   (adjective)

Exercise 34   **Sentence combining: Subordinate clauses, p. 30**

Possible answer:

1. Moviegoers expect <u>that movie sequels should be as exciting as the
   original films.</u>

Exercise 35   **Identifying sentence types, p. 31**

1. <u>Joseph Pulitzer endowed the Pulitzer Prizes.</u> [Simple.]

Exercise 36   **Sentence combining: Sentence types, p. 31**

Possible answer:

1.   Recycling takes time, but it reduces garbage in landfills.

Exercise 37   **Using irregular verbs, p. 32**

1.   The world population has <u>grown</u> by two-thirds of a billion people in less than a decade. [Past participle.]

Exercise 38   **Distinguishing *sit/set*, *lie/lay*, *rise/raise*, p. 33**

1.   Yesterday afternoon the child <u>lay</u> down for a nap.

Exercise 39   **Using *-s* and *-ed* verb endings, p. 34**

A teacher sometimes <u>asks</u> too much of a student.

Exercise 40   **Using helping verbs, p. 34**

1.   Each year thousands of new readers <u>have</u> been discovering Agatha Christie's mysteries.

Exercise 41   **Revising: Helping verbs plus main verbs (ESL), p. 35**

1.   A report from the Bureau of the Census has <u>confirmed</u> a widening gap between rich and poor.

Exercise 42   **Revising: Verbs plus gerunds or infinitives (ESL), p. 36**

1.   A program called HELP Wanted tries to make citizens <u>take</u> action on behalf of American competitiveness.

Exercise 43   Revising: Verbs plus particles (ESL), p. 37

1. American movies treat everything from going out (I) with someone to making up (S) an ethnic identity, but few people (a) look into their significance.

Exercise 44   Adjusting tense sequence: Past or past perfect tense, p. 38

1. Diaries that Adolf Hitler was supposed to have written had surfaced in Germany.

Exercise 45   Revising: Tense sequence with conditional sentences (ESL), p. 39

1. When an athlete turns professional, he or she commits to a grueling regimen of mental and physical training.

Exercise 46   Using verb tenses in indirect quotations (ESL), p. 40

1. Lamb cited Coleridge's observation that a man could not have a pure mind who refused apple-dumplings.

Exercise 47   Revising: Subjunctive mood, p. 41

1. If John Hawkins had known of the dangerous side effects of smoking tobacco, would he have introduced the dried plant to England in 1565?

Exercise 48   Converting between active and passive voices, p. 42

1. When engineers built the Eiffel Tower in 1889, the French thought it was ugly.

Exercise 49   Revising: Subject-verb agreement, p. 43

1. Weinstein & Associates <u>is</u> a consulting firm that <u>tries</u> to make business-people laugh.

Exercise 50   Choosing between subjective and objective pronouns, p. 44

1. Jody and <u>I</u> had been hunting for jobs.

Exercise 51   Choosing between *who* and *whom*, p. 45

1. The school administrators suspended Jurgen, <u>whom</u> they suspected of setting the fire.

Exercise 52   Sentence combining: *Who* versus *whom*, p. 46

Possible answer:

1. Some children <u>who have undetected hearing problems</u> may do poorly in school.

Exercise 53   Choosing between subjective and objective pronouns, p. 47

1. Obtaining enough protein is important to <u>us</u> vegetarians.

Exercise 54   Revising: Case, p. 48

Written four thousand years ago, *The Epic of Gilgamesh* tells of the friendship of Gilgamesh and Enkidu. Gilgamesh was a bored king who [correct] his people thought was too harsh.

Exercise 55   Revising: Pronoun-antecedent agreement, p. 49

1. Each girl raised in a Mexican American family in the Rio Grande
    Valley of Texas hopes that one day <u>she</u> will be given a *quinceañera* party
    for <u>her</u> fifteenth birthday.

Exercise 56   Revising: Ambiguous and remote pronoun reference,
                p. 50

1. There is a difference between the heroes of the twentieth century and
    the heroes of earlier times: <u>twentieth-century heroes</u> have flaws in their
    characters.

Exercise 57   Revising: Indefinite and inappropriate pronoun
                reference, p. 51

1. "Life begins at forty" is a cliché many people live by, and this <u>saying</u>
    may well be true.

Exercise 58   Revising: Pronoun reference, p. 52

   In Charlotte Bronte's *Jane Eyre,* <u>Jane</u> is a shy young woman <u>who</u> takes a
job as governess.

Exercise 59   Revising: Adjectives and adverbs, p. 53

1. King George III of England declared Samuel Johnson <u>suitable</u> for a
    pension.

Exercise 60   Revising: Comparatives and superlatives, p. 54

1. Charlotte was the <u>oldest</u> of the three Brontë sisters, all of whom were
    novelists.

Exercise 61   Revising: Present and past participles (ESL), p. 55

1. Several critics found Alice Walker's *The Color Purple* to be a <u>fascinating</u> book.

Exercise 62   Revising: Articles (ESL), p. 56

From <u>the</u> native American Indians who migrated fro<u>m As</u>ia 20,000 years ago to <u>the</u> new arrivals who now come b<u>y p</u>lane, <u>the</u> United States is <u>a</u> nation of foreigners.

Exercise 63   Revising: Misplaced clauses and phrases, p. 57

1. Women have contributed <u>much of great value to </u>knowledge and culture.

Exercise 64   Revising: Placement of adverbs and adjectives (ESL), p. 58

1. Some years ago Detroit cars were <u>often</u> praised.

Exercise 65   Revising: Dangling modifiers, p. 59

Possible answer:

1. After <u>Andrew Jackson had accomplished</u> many deeds of valor, <u>his</u> fame led to his election to the Presidency in 1828 and 1832.

Exercise 66   Sentence combining: Placing modifiers, p. 60

Possible answer:

1. As evening falls in the Central American rain forests, the tungara frogs begin their croaking chorus.

Exercise 67   **Revising: Misplaced and dangling modifiers, p. 61**

Possible revision:

<u>Several nights a week</u>, Central American tungara frogs silence their mating croaks.

Exercise 68   **Identifying and revising sentence fragments, p. 61**

1. Lacks a subject and a verb.
    Complete: <u>An article</u> about vandalism against works of art <u>was</u> interesting.
    Combined: In an interesting article about vandalism against works of art, <u>the author says the vandals' motives vary widely</u>.

2. Lacks a verb.
    Complete: The motives of the vandals <u>vary</u> widely.

    Combined: The motives of the vandals varying widely, <u>researchers can make few generalizations</u>.

Exercise 69   **Revising sentence fragments, p. 63**

Possible answers:

1. Human beings who perfume themsel<u>ves are</u> not much different from other animals.
2. Animals as varied as insects and dogs release *pheromo<u>nes,</u>* chemicals that signal other animals.

Exercise 70   **Revising: Sentence fragments, p. 64**

Possible revision:

Baby red-eared slider turtles are brightly colored, <u>with</u> bold patterns on their yellowish undershells <u>that</u> serve as a warning to predators.

Exercise 71   Identifying and revising comma splices, p. 65

Possible answers:

1. Money has a long history. It goes back at least as far as the earliest
    records.
    Money has a long history that goes back at least as far as the earliest
    records.

Exercise 72   Identifying and revising fused sentences, p. 66

Possible answers:

1. Throughout history money and religion were closely linked because
    there was little distinction between government and religion.
    Throughout history money and religion were closely linked, for there
    was little distinction between government and religion.

Exercise 73   Sentence combining: Comma splices and fused
                   sentences, p. 67

Possible answer:

1. The exact origin of paper money is unknown because it has not sur-
    vived as coins, shells, and other durable objects have.

Exercise 74   Revising: Comma splices and fused sentences, p. 68

All those parents who urged their children to eat broccoli were right;
for the vegetable really is healthful.

Exercise 75   Revising: Sentences mixed in grammar or meaning, p. 68

Possible answer:

1. A hurricane occurs when the winds in a tropical depression rotate
    counterclockwise at more than seventy-four miles per hour.

Exercise 76   Revising: Repeated sentence parts (ESL), p. 69

1.   Global warming is caused by the gradual erosion of the ozone layer that
     protects the earth from the sun.

Exercise 77   Revising: Periods, p. 71

1.   The instructor asked when Plato wrote *The Republic.*

Exercise 78   Revising: End punctuation, p. 71

     When visitors first arrive in Hawaii, they often encounter an unexpect-
ed language barrier.

Exercise 79   Using the comma with linked main clauses, p. 72

1.   Parents once automatically gave their children the father's surname,
     but some no longer do.

Exercise 80   Using the comma with introductory elements, p. 73

1.   [Sentence correct.]
2.   Because it is sudden and apparently well coordinated, the movement of
     flocks and schools has seemed to be directed by a leader.

Exercise 81   Using the comma with nonessential elements, p. 74

1.   Italians insist that Marco Polo, the thirteenth-century explorer, did not
     import pasta from China.

Exercise 82   Sentence combining: Commas with nonessential elements, p. 75

Possible answer:

1. American colonists first imported pasta from the English, who had discovered it as tourists in Italy.

Exercise 83   Using the comma with series and coordinate adjectives, p. 76

1. Shoes with high heels originated to protect feet from the mud, garbage, and animal waste in the streets.

Exercise 84   Using the comma with dates, addresses, place names, numbers, p. 77

1. The festival will hold a benefit dinner and performance on March 10, 2002, in Asheville.

Exercise 85   Using the comma or semicolon with quotations, p. 78

1. [Sentence correct.]
2. "I think of the open-ended writing process as a voyage in two stages," Elbow says.

Exercise 86   Revising: Needless or misused commas, p. 79

1. Nearly 32 million US residents_speak a first language other than English.

Exercise 87   Revising: Commas, p. 79

Ellis Island, New York, has reopened for business, but now the customers are tourists, not immigrants.

Exercise 88   **Using the semicolon between main clauses, p. 81**

1. Music is a form of communication like language; the basic elements, however, are not letters but notes.

Exercise 89   **Revising: Misused or overused semicolons, p. 82**

1. The main religion in India is Hinduism, a way of life as well as a theology and philosophy.

Exercise 90   **Revising: Semicolons, p. 83**

The set, sounds, and actors in the movie captured the essence of horror films. The set was ideal: dark, deserted streets; trees dipping their branches over the sidewalks; mist hugging the ground and creeping up to meet the trees; looming shadows of unlighted, turreted houses,

Exercise 91   **Revising: Colons, p. 84**

1. In the remote parts of many Third World countries, simple signs mark human habitation: a dirt path, a few huts, smoke from a campfire.

Exercise 92   **Forming possessives with the apostrophe, p. 85**

1. In the myths of the ancient Greeks, the goddesses' roles vary widely.

Exercise 93   **Using the apostrophe with some plurals, p. 85**

1. 7's or 7s

Exercise 94   **Revising: Apostrophes, p. 86**

Landlocked Chad is among the world's most troubled countries.

Exercise 95   Revising: Quotation marks, p. 86

In one class we talked about a passage from "I Have a Dream," the speech delivered by Martin Luther King, Jr., on the steps of the Lincoln Memorial on August 28, 1963:

Exercise 96   Revising: Punctuation, p. 88

Brewed coffee is the most widely consumed beverage in the world. The trade in coffee beans alone amounts to well over $6,000,000,000 a year, and the total volume of beans traded exceeds 4,250,000 tons a year.

Exercise 97   Using spelling rules, p. 91

a. brief   b. malicious   c. implies   d. repairing   e. piles

Exercise 98   Using hyphens in compound words, p. 92

1. [Correct.]
2. de-escalate

Exercise 99   Revising: Capitals, p. 93

1. San Antonio, Texas, is a thriving city in the Southwest.

Exercise 100   Revising: Underlining or Italics, p. 94

1. Of the many Vietnam veterans who are writers, Oliver Stone is perhaps the most famous for writing and directing the films Platoon and Born on the Fourth of July.

Exercise 101   Revising: Abbreviations, p. 96

1. In the September 17, 1993, issue of *Science* magazine, Virgil L. Sharpton discusses a theory that could help explain the extinction of dinosaurs.

Exercise 102   Revising: Numbers, p. 97

1. The planet Saturn is <u>900</u> million miles, or nearly <u>1.5 billion</u> kilometers, from Earth.

Exercise 103   Evaluating and synthesizing sources, p. 99

The key similarities and differences are these:

Similarities: Nadelmann and Posey agree that crackdowns or penalties do not stop the drug trade. Nadelmann and Runkle agree that the drug trade affects the young, who are most impressionable.

Differences: Nadelmann maintains that the illegal drug trade does more to entice youths to drugs than do the drugs themselves, whereas Runkle maintains that the illegality discourages youths from using prohibited drugs. Posey, in contrast to Runkle, claims that penalties do nothing to discourage drug abusers.

Exercise 104   Summarizing and paraphrasing, p. 100

Possible summary:

Eisinger *at al.*, 44

Federalism, unlike a unitary system, allows the states autonomy. Its strength and its weakness – which are in balance – lie in the regional differences it permits.

Exercise 105   Combining summary, paraphrase, and direct quotation, p. 101

Possible answer:

Farb, 107

Speakers at parties often "unconsciously duel" in conversations in order to assert "dominance" over others.

Exercise 106   Recognizing plagiarism, p. 102

1.   Plagiarized: takes phrases directly from the original without quotation
       marks.

Exercise 108   Writing MLA works-cited entries, p. 104

1.   Kim, Jocelyn, "Credit and Consumer Confidence."

       <u>Adaptation</u> to Change 12.4 (1998) : 101-06